THE CHOICE OF WORDS

THE CHOICE OF WORDS

A BOOK OF SYNONYMS
WITH EXPLANATIONS

by
V. H. COLLINS

You are light as dreams,
Tough as oak,
Precious as gold,
As poppies and corn,
Or an old cloak.
EDWARD THOMAS, "Words"

1724

LONGMANS, GREEN AND CO
LONDON ◇ NEW YORK ◇ TORONTO

LONGMANS, GREEN AND CO LTD
6 & 7 CLIFFORD STREET LONDON W 1

ALSO AT MELBOURNE AND CAPE TOWN

LONGMANS, GREEN AND CO INC
55 FIFTH AVENUE NEW YORK 3

LONGMANS, GREEN AND CO
215 VICTORIA STREET TORONTO 1

ORIENT LONGMANS LTD
BOMBAY CALCUTTA MADRAS

First published 1952

PRINTED IN GREAT BRITAIN
BY WESTERN PRINTING SERVICES LTD., BRISTOL

TO
HELEN THOMAS

CONTENTS

PREFACE

THE purpose of this book is to throw light on contemporary English usage by giving as concisely as possible explanations of the distinction in meaning, often slight, of a number of selected synonyms, especially words whose meanings are most commonly confused. The words given are generally dealt with only in relation to their synonyms. Occasionally, however, when a word is used in more than one sense, it has been thought desirable, after dealing with its synonymous use, to mention briefly one or more other meanings.

Synonyms in the narrowest sense are words whose meaning is so identical that one can always be substituted for the other without change in the effect of the sentence in which it is done. W. H. Fowler says that whether any such perfect synonyms exist is doubtful, and that at any rate they are extremely rare. Thus he cites **gorse** and **furze**, and points out that, if it is a fact that one is more often used than the other, or is prevalent in different geographical regions or social circles, the exchange between them can alter the effect on hearers or readers, and synonymity is not perfect. For practical purposes, however, this consideration can generally be ignored, and in a wider sense synonyms can be taken to mean two or more words that in one or other of their acceptations are usually able to be substituted for each other without affecting the meaning of the sentence. Misapprehensions of the degree in which words are synonymous is responsible for much bad speaking and writing, and to appreciate the difference between words that are not properly synonymous at all, or between those that are only partially synonymous, is of the utmost importance for a clear, precise, and vigorous style.

A complication in language is that many words are synonymous with one or more words in one sense and in a given context but are not so in another sense and in a different context. To quote Fowler again, it does not matter whether we say a word has "two senses" or "two meanings." To that extent **sense** and **meaning** are synonymous. If, however, "He is a man of sense" is rewritten "He is a man of meaning," it becomes clear that **sense** and **meaning** are not perfectly synonymous. Consequently in the course of the explanations it has often been necessary to make some such statement as that "In many contexts the two words are interchangeable," or to use some such qualifying phrase as that a given word "generally" has a certain implication.

In a book of this sort it is inevitable that, besides the definitions of distinctions between words, with illustrative sentences, there should frequently be mention of misuses, and discussion of new words and the new use of old words: most of them unnecessary, loose, or for other reasons undesirable; a few that are useful; a few about which judgment must be suspended whether possibly or probably they will eventually become established.

Thanks are due to many friends and acquaintances: to Mrs. Helen Thomas for encouragement and for detailed help on many matters; to H. A. Treble, whose recent death I deeply deplore, for many alterations resulting from his criticisms, both destructive and constructive; to Miss Alyse Gregory, Mr. G. V. Carey, Mr. D. M. Davin, Mr. Bethel Jacobs, Dr. A. Jackson, Mr. K. W. Luckhurst, Mr. Anthony Martienssen, Professor A. A. Matheson, Mr. C. Matheson, Mr. Raymond Mortimer, Rev. J. H. Powell, Mr. Russell Scott, Mr. L. W. Taylor, Mr. Philip Wayne, Mr. Louis Wilkinson. For help on some words, and for permission for some quotations, for which acknowledgements appear in the body of the book, I am indebted to the late Earl Wavell, Mrs. Faith Compton Mackenzie, Mr. E. M. Forster, the Proprietors of *The Times* and of *Punch*. To Mr. M. Alderton Pink I am obliged for the loan, to a stranger, when his book was out of print and the British Museum's copy was not available, of *Illustrations of English Synonyms*, with its interesting collection of sentences.

It is almost unnecessary to say that I have constantly consulted the Oxford Dictionaries and H. W. Fowler's *Dictionary of Modern English Usage*. The Delegates of the Clarendon Press have given generous leave for the numerous references to and quotations from these books. The excellent little handbook, *An ABC of English Usage*, by H. A. Treble and G. H. Vallins, has been most useful, as has also been Sir Alan Herbert's *What a Word!* with its hilarious wisdom. From Sir Ernest Gowers I have been privileged to receive letters on points in his book *Plain Words*, about which I had written to him.

Generally it has been thought more convenient to cite the *Concise Oxford Dictionary* than the two larger Oxford Dictionaries.

The following abbreviations are used:

C.O.D.=*The Concise Oxford Dictionary of Current Usage* by H. W. Fowler and F. G. Fowler (Third Edition with Revised Addenda, 1946);

M.E.U.=*A Dictionary of Modern English Usage* by H. W. Fowler (Reprint of 1937 with corrections).

LIST OF GROUPS

1 abuse, invective, obloquy, vituperation, scurrility
2 admission, admittance
3 alibi, defence, excuse
4 ambiguous, equivocal
5 among, amongst, amid, amidst
6 answer, reply, rejoinder, retort, repartee, riposte
7 anticipate, expect
8 antipathetic, allergic
9 anyhow, anyway
10 arrival, advent
11 as, while, whereas
12 authentic, genuine
13 barbarism, barbarity, barbarousness
14 base, basis
15 begin, commence, start, initiate
16 benignant, benign, benevolent, beneficent
17 bereavement, loss
18 blitz, attack, damage
19 bloom, blossom, flower
20 Briton, Britisher
21 brothers, brethren
22 brutish, brutal, beastly, bestial
23 burlesque, skit, parody, caricature, travesty, lampoon
24 call, describe, term, designate, denominate
25 capacity, ability, capability, aptitude
26 category, class, division
27 ceiling, limit
28 ceremonial, ceremonious
29 change, alter
30 cheerful, cheery
31 childlike, childish
32 classical, classic
33 client, customer
34 colourful, vivid, interesting
35 commonplace, platitude, truism, axiom
36 comparatively, relatively, rather, somewhat, etc.
37 conceal, hide, secrete

38 conception, concept, idea
39 concourse, crowd
40 confirm, verify, check, check up, check up on, corroborate, endorse
41 conservative, moderate, cautious
42 contact, meet
43 contagious, infectious
44 contain, include, comprise, consist
45 contemplate, meditate, premeditate
46 constantly, continually, continuously, perpetually, incessantly
47 continuance, continuation, continuity, continuousness
48 contract, catch, get
49 controversial, contentious
50 corpse, carcase
51 counterpart, opposite number
52 credit, credence
53 crime, immorality, vice, misdemeanour, felony, sin, wicked-
54 criticism, appreciation, evaluation, appraisal, critique
55 criticize, blame, condemn, censure, reprove, rebuke, reprimand, upbraid, reproach, scold, chide
56 cry, weep, sob, wail
57 cryptic, mysterious
58 deduce, infer, gather, understand
59 deficient, defective
60 definite, definitive
61 definitely, certainly, undoubtedly, surely
62 delightful, delicious, delectable
63 deny, repudiate
64 depreciate, disparage, decry, denigrate, debunk,
65 depression, dejection, despondency, melancholy
66 derive, originate, stem
67 designation, description, term, name, title
68 deteriorate, worsen, degenerate
69 difference, differentiation
70 different, diverse
71 difficult, hard
72 difficulty, quandary, dilemma
73 disapprove, depreciate
74 discover, find, find out, ascertain

75 disinterested, uninterested, impartial, unbiased
76 disposal, disposition
77 distinct, distinctive
78 dividend, profit, advantage
79 divagate, digress, stray
80 doctor, physician, surgeon
81 doff, take off; don, put on
82 dress, frock, robe, gown, costume
83 drunk, drunken, intoxicated, inebriated, tipsy
84 eatable, edible
85 edifice, building
86 efficient, effective, efficacious, effectual
87 egoist, egotist
88 end, finish, conclude, terminate, complete
89 endeavour, try, strive, attempt, seek
90 entry, entrance
91 epic, heroic
92 equalitarian, egalitarian
93 ere, before
94 Esq., Mr.
95 essential, necessary, requisite
96 evacuate, empty, remove
97 exceptional, unusual, abnormal, anomalous, morbid
98 exclusive, select
99 executive, official, officer
100 exiguous, small
101 expensive, dear, costly
102 experiment, experimentation
103 exploit, work, use, utilize
104 extremely, exceedingly, excessively
105 face, countenance, visage, physiognomy
106 face, face up to
107 facile, easy
108 factor, fact
109 famous, celebrated, noted, notorious, notable, noteworthy, eminent
110 fatal, fateful
111 fault, failing, foible
112 feature, portray, depict, describe
113 female, feminine, womanly, womanish, effeminate

114 few, some, number, several, divers, sundry
115 fewer, less
116 finally, ultimately
117 fluctuate, vacillate
118 following, after
119 foolish, stupid, silly
120 forcible, forceful
121 foreword, preface, introduction
122 forward, dispatch, transmit, send
123 friendship, friendliness, amity
124 frighten, terrify, alarm, intimidate, scare
125 function, act, work, operate
126 garret, attic, loft
127 give, present, donate, gift, bequest
128 glance, glimpse
129 global, globe, world
130 gourmand, gourmet
131 gratis, gratuitously, free
132 Greek, Grecian
133 guarantee, agree, ensure, promise, assure
134 habit, custom
135 hanged, hung
136 happen, occur, develop, eventuate, materialize, transpire
137 happening, event, occurrence, incident, episode, eventuality, contingency, development
138 hectic, exciting, wild
139 help, aid, assist, succour
140 hither, here
141 hopeless, desperate
142 horrible, awful, terrible, dreadful, fearful, frightful, horrid, terrific, tremendous
143 human, human being
144 hypocrite, dissembler, dissimulator
145 if, though, although, but
146 illegible, unreadable, indecipherable, undecipherable
147 illness, sickness, disease, malady, ailment, indisposition
148 immediately, instantly, directly, instantaneously, forthwith, straightway, straightaway, right away, right off
149 impecunious, indigent, poor
150 impertinent, insolent, impudent, saucy, cheeky

151 implement, complete, fulfil
152 imply, insinuate, connote, infer, mean
153 impossible, intolerable, unworkable, incredible
154 impostor, charlatan, quack
155 imprison, incarcerate, intern
156 in, at
157 inability, disability
158 incidentally, passingly
159 incredible, unbelievable
160 individual, person
161 inquire, ask, demand
162 insure, ensure, assure
163 intense, intensive
164 intermediary, mediate
165 interrogate, question
166 intrigue, interest, puzzle
167 involve, entail
168 irony, sarcasm, satire
169 irritating, annoying, exasperating, aggravating
170 issue, supply
171 jocose, jocular, facetious, comic, comical, funny
172 judicial, judicious
173 judge, adjudicate
174 kill, slay, murder, massacre, slaughter, assassinate, decimate
175 knowledgeable, well-informed
176 late, belated
177 latest, last, latter, late
178 lazy, idle, indolent, slothful
179 lengthy, long
180 letter, note, communication, favour, epistle, missive, screed
181 libel, slander, calumny
182 lifelong, livelong
183 like, as
184 likely, probable; likely, probably
185 limited, small
186 liquidate, eliminate, remove
187 list, include, mention
188 locality, place, district
189 look, gaze, peer
190 luncheon, lunch

191 magician, wizard, sorcerer, conjurer, illusionist, juggler
192 majority, most
193 male, masculine, manly, mannish, virile
194 malignant, malign, malevolent, maleficient, malicious
195 man, gentleman; woman, lady
196 manned, manned up
197 many, numerous
198 maybe, perhaps
199 melody, tune
200 memory, remembrance, recollection, reminiscence
201 mental, mad, insane
202 mentality, mind
203 meticulous, scrupulous, punctilious, careful
204 minimize, belittle, lessen, reduce
205 minute, second, moment, instant
206 mishap, accident
207 miss, lose
208 mistake, error, fallacy
209 moderate, mediocre, modest
210 modest, diffident, shy
211 motivate, activate, actuate
212 mutual, common, reciprocal
213 myth, legend, fable, parable, allegory
214 near, near-by, neighbouring, nigh
215 need, requirement, demand, exigence, exigency
216 never, not
217 nice, pleasant
218 nil, nothing
219 nostalgia, yearning
220 number, song, tune
221 object, demur
222 oblivious, forgetful, unmindful,
223 obtain, procure, secure, acquire, get, gain, win
224 Occident, West; Orient, East
225 often, frequently
226 old, elderly, senescent, aged, ancient, veteran, senile, anti-
    quated.
227 onslaught, assault, attack
228 optimistic, hopeful, sanguine
229 order, command, instruction, direction, directive, injunction

230 ornamental, ornate, decorative
231 otherwise, not
232 overall, total
233 pact, compact
234 painful, poignant
235 painter, artist, artiste
236 part, portion, share, proportion, percentage
237 partake, participate, share
238 pass, die, expire, decease, perish; passing, death, decease, demise
239 pecuniary, monetary
240 people, persons, folk
241 permission, consent, leave, permit
242 permit, consent, let, allow
243 perpetrate, commit
244 person, personage, personality, individuality, character party
245 personally, myself
246 personnel, staff, employees
247 peruse, read
248 pessimistic, hopeless
249 phenomenal, remarkable, extraordinary
250 piteous, pitiful, pitiable
251 place, put
252 plan, scheme, blue-print
253 polish, burnish
254 polite, courteous
255 politic, expedient
256 possession, advantage, asset
257 possible, feasible, practicable, practical, realistic
258 practically, almost, nearly, virtually
259 praise, eulogy, eulogium, encomium
260 preciseness, precision
261 prejudice, damage
262 prerequisite, precondition, condition
263 presume, assume
264 presumption, assumption, hypothesis, postulate
265 pretend, effect, purport, claim
266 pride, haughtiness, arrogance, vanity, conceit
267 primary, prime, premier, chief, first, primal

[7]

268 proceed, go, come
269 product, produce
270 proffer, tender, offer
271 proposition, proposal, plan
272 protagonist, champion
273 prudent, prudential
274 psychological, suitable
275 pupil, student, scholar, trainee
276 puppet, marionette
277 purchase, buy
278 quiescent, quiet
279 quote, cite
280 reaction, response
281 ready, prepared, willing
282 realize, know
283 really, actually, positively, absolutely, literally, veritably
284 recondition, renovate
285 recriminations, accusations, charges
286 redundant, superfluous, unnecessary
287 refer, allude, advert
288 regarding, respecting, concerning, anent, re
289 register, record, show
290 regret, be sorry, deplore, lament
291 rehabilitation, restoration
292 remark, comment, observation
293 remember, recollect, recall, reminisce
294 remittance, money
295 remove, take away
296 render, make
297 render, sing, play
298 repast, collation, meal
299 repeat, reiterate, iterate
300 reside, dwell, live
301 residence, mansion, abode, domicile, dwelling, house, home
302 resort, recourse, resource
303 result, effect, consequence, aftermath, repercussion
304 result, accrue
305 resume, continue
306 retaliation, reprisal
307 reticent, taciturn, secretive

308 retreat, retire, withdraw
309 retrieve, recover, regain, get back
310 reveal, display, manifest, exhibit, disclose, evince
311 rich, wealthy, opulent, affluent
312 ride, drive
313 room, rooms, accommodation, apartment, lodging
314 sabotage, damage
315 same, it, this, them, these
316 save, except
317 say, state, assert, affirm, declare, aver, announce, proclaim,
   intimate, indicate, maintain, claim, allege
318 Scotch, Scottish, Scot, Scots
319 section, cross-section, sample
320 see, perceive, discern, descry, espy
321 seek, search
322 sell, dispose
323 sense, feel
324 sensual, sensuous
325 service, maintain
326 serviette, napkin
327 shadow, shade
328 shall, will; should, would
329 shambles, slaughter-house
330 ship, boat, vessel
331 short, brief, concise, succinct, terse
332 show-down, test
333 shut, close
334 sincerely, truly, faithfully
335 slogan, watchword, motto, catchword
336 smell, odour, scent, perfume, fragrance, aroma, bouquet
337 solecism, mistake, error, catachresis, jargon, howler
338 be sorry, be afraid, fear, regret
339 specially, especially, particularly
340 speech, harangue, tirade
341 spot, piece
342 stage, arrange
343 stagger, spread
344 steal, purloin, pilfer, filch, thieve, rob
345 step up, increase
346 stimulus, stimulant

347 stoic, stoical
348 stomach, belly, abdomen, tummy
349 stop, cease, desist, intermit, discontinue
350 stress, emphasize
351 superlative, excellent
352 supplementary, complementary, additional
353 surprise, astonish, amaze, astound
354 surrender, capitulate
355 suspension, suspense
356 sustain, suffer
357 sweat, perspiration
358 synthetic, artificial, imitation, ersatz
359 talk, conversation, converse, recourse
360 tall, high, lofty
361 target, objective
362 tell, inform, advise, acquaint, apprise
363 that, who, whom, which
364 their, his, her
365 think, consider, feel
366 thrash, beat up, beat
367 throw, cast
368 top, summit, peak, apex
369 towards, toward
370 transport, transportation
371 trick, manœuvre, stratagem, subterfuge
372 triumphant, triumphal
373 try, try out, test, test out
374 typist, typewriter
375 understand, comprehend, apprehend
376 undoubtedly, doubtless, indubitably
377 undue, excessive
378 unilateral, independent
379 unique, singular, exceptional
380 unsophisticated, inexperienced, naïve, artless
381 unthinkable, inconceivable
382 use, usage
383 various, varied
384 venue, meeting-place, rendezvous
385 veracious, truthful, true
386 very, much, greatly, etc.

387 viand, victual, food
388 view, opinion, view-point, standpoint
389 visualize, envisage
390 vocation, avocation
391 voice, express
392 volume, tome, title, book
393 wage, salary, fee, remuneration, emolument, stipend, bonus, gratuity, tip, honorarium, payment
394 wake, waken, awake, awaken
395 washing, ablution
396 weighty, heavy
397 wood, forest
398 woollen, woolly
399 write, send, address
400 young, youthful, juvenile, puerile

1   ABUSE, INVECTIVE, VITUPERATION, OBLOQUY, SCURRILITY

These words in their roughly synonymous use imply bitter attack on conduct or character.

abuse is the general working word. As contrasted with **invective, abuse** is used mostly for private reproach or condemnation; **invective** for studied and public denunciation in print or in oratory. **abuse** generally carries with it the idea of accusation expressed in violent and coarse terms, whereas **invective** may be polished and dignified in style. Dr. Johnson said "Invective is an ornament of debate, but insolence is not invective". Celebrated examples of **invective** are Cicero's *Philippic Orations* against Mark Antony and Burke's opening speech in the impeachment of Warren Hastings. Few attacks by contemporary politicians on their opponents rise to the level of **invective**, but many degenerate into **abuse**; and in our private lives most of us have been the victims of **abuse**.

vituperation is a long-winded alternative for the shorter and simpler word **abuse**, but perhaps its sound and very length convey the idea of a torrential flow of **abuse**.

defamation can refer both to the utterance of charges against a person and to their effect in injuring his reputation.

obloquy is commonly used with reference, not to **abuse** as an active thing, but to the condition of being, or having been, spoken against, sometimes involving lasting disgrace. "Warren Hastings said at his trial that nations of India of all ranks had come forward unsolicited to clear his name from the obloquy with which it was loaded."

scurrility implies charges, generally of debased conduct, expressed in coarse language. "The scurrility of his methods was typically expressed by his description of his opponents as 'lower than vermin.' "

The uses of the verbs **abuse, inveigh** (against), **vituperate, defame,** and the adjectives **abusive, vituperative, defamatory** correspond with those of the nouns. (In future throughout this book, when the uses of nouns have been dealt with, it will not as a rule be thought necessary to refer to the uses of corresponding verbs, adjectives, adverbs; nor conversely.)

ADMISSION, ADMITTANCE   2

admission, for being allowed to enter (usually a place), is the commonly used word, and it has today almost entirely displaced **admittance,** which is now restricted to a few idiomatic uses, e.g. "No admittance except on business".

ALIBI, DEFENCE, EXCUSE   3

alibi (by derivation a Latin adverb="at another place"), which until recent years never meant anything except a plea by a person that, when an alleged act happened, he was elsewhere, is now being used for any grounds for **defence** against a charge, and in even more slipshod senses with the meaning of **excuse.** "The excuse that our troubles are all due to a shortage of dollars is nonsense, and is an alibi for foolish planning." "His subsequent imprecations seem to have been better calculated to establish his alibi for the future than to produce effective action." I have been told that the first occasion on which this usage appeared in print was in a report in an American newspaper of a prize-fight where the beaten man, in admitting a fair defeat, was alleged to have said "I have no alibi". The usage is common in French, among even good writers, as for example, André Gide.

AMBIGUOUS, EQUIVOCAL   4

Both words have the sense "of double meaning." Distinctions are as follows. **ambiguous** can imply intentional or unintentional obscurity; **equivocal** implies that the obscurity is intentional, to confuse or deceive. **ambiguous** is restricted to what is spoken or written, and to a person; **equivocal** applies also to action.

ambiguous has the corresponding noun **ambiguity**. **equivocal** has two corresponding nouns: **equivocation**, synonymous with **ambiguity**, and **equivocator** (a person who is **equivocal**); and a verb, **equivocate**.

5   AMONG, AMONGST, AMID, AMIDST

among and **amongst** are used of position in relation to other persons or things, and must therefore be followed by a plural word. "He was only one among (or amongst) many to be defrauded by this rascal." Hence "among (or amongst) the guests", but not "among (or amongst) the crowd", even though "crowd" is a collective noun implying a plural. *M.E.U.* suggests that for euphony **amongst** is more usual than **among** before vowels.

amid and **amidst** refer to position in relation to a single thing and must therefore be followed by a singular word. "Amidst the panic around him he remained cool."

6   ANSWER, REPLY, REJOINDER, RETORT, REPARTEE, RIPOSTE

answer and **reply** (closely synonymous) are the ordinary working nouns. **riposte**, which in its primary sense is a fencing term, for a quick thrust given after parrying a lunge, means in a general sense, with reference to action, a counter-stroke; with reference to spoken words, an incisive answer. This too is the meaning of **rejoinder, retort** (a bitter answer), **repartee** (a witty answer). **rejoinder** can refer also to what is written.

There are corresponding verbs to all the nouns, but to **riposte** is rare, and to **repartee** is rarer still.

The primary and distinctive meaning of to **anticipate** (Latin *capere*="to take", *ante*="beforehand") is to **forestall**: to take action before somebody else can do something, or before something occurs. "He anticipated her design by placing himself between her and the door." "I do not ask the Foreign Secretary to make a statement that would anticipate answers he may be giving tomorrow." "Knowing he was in difficulties I decided to anticipate the date of payment due to him by three weeks and I thereby gained his lasting gratitude." "The Government has anticipated formal conclusion of the fact by sending the General to London to develop American contributions to military aid." "In André Gide's *Fruits of the Earth*, published more than forty years ago, there are statements that seem to anticipate the opinions today associated with Sartre."

To **expect** is to believe that something will happen, is happening, has happened. "I expect him at six o'clock." "I expect to return home next week." "I expect he arrived yesterday."

Journalese with its craving for long words has adopted **anticipate** as a synonym of **expect**. "I anticipated his arrival tomorrow." "We anticipated that he would refuse the offer." Dickens helped to popularize the misuse, as he did in other debasements of the language: see e.g. **mutual** (212), **aggravate** (169), **phenomenon** (249).

The nearest attempt I have heard to defend this use of **anticipate** is the argument that **expect** implies positive belief that a thing will happen; **anticipate** only an opinion that it may do so. But if "I anticipate it will rain tomorrow" means "I think it will rain tomorrow", why not say so? The misuse is to be especially deplored because, apart from cluttering up the language with a superfluous and long synonym, for a shorter and established word with the same meaning, it tends to banish from the language a use of **anticipate** that is distinct and useful. Compare **aggravating** (169) and **protagonist** (272).

A similar objection applies to the noun **anticipation** when it means merely **expectation**. "Our anticipation that the shares would rise was disappointed." It does not apply, however, when, as in some contexts the senses of **forestall** and **expect** overlap. "In anticipation of showers we took our macintoshes." "We rode up those hills with zestful anticipation of the fine free-wheel descent on the other side."

8   ANTIPATHETIC, ALLERGIC

allergic is strictly a medical term for "reacting differently to a subsequent inoculation or treatment with the same thing". With a perverted extension of this somewhat complicated sense it has come lately to be used as a synonym of **antipathetic**: "having a constitutional or settled aversion". *C.O.D.* gives as an example "allergic to blondes". In a recent novel a woman is said "always to have been very allergic to this man", and in the publisher's notice of another novel a male character is described as being "so allergic to conventional values as to find a sardonic delight in flouting them". Time will show whether good writers will be "allergic" to this use of the word.

9   ANYHOW, ANYWAY

anyhow and **anyway** are (*a*) pure adverbs meaning "in any way whatever", often with the implication that the manner is careless, haphazard, unmethodical: "She was in such a hurry that she packed the case anyhow." "You can arrange them anyway" (in any order); (*b*) conjunctival adverbs meaning "in any case", "at all events", "at any rate", "however that may be": "Anyhow (or anyway) the immediate danger was now averted"; "Anyhow (or anyway) I'll let you know what he says". The conjunctival use of both words, which is more modern than the adverbial use, has still a somewhat colloquial ring, but on account of the convenience of single words as alternatives for phrases of three or four words—"in any case", etc.—it is now fairly common in the written language.

ARRIVAL, ADVENT   10

advent is restricted to an **arrival** of some solemnity. We speak of the **arrival** of a train, of a visitor, of spring; of the **advent** of Christmas.

AS, WHILE, WHILST, WHEREAS,   11
THOUGH, ALTHOUGH

In their synonymous relation to each other **while** refers to the whole time during which something happens; **as** refers to a particular moment. "While I was in Scotland the weather was fine"; "As I was walking along the drive a dog flew at me." Apart from its original use as a conjunction of time, **while** has a legitimate use in contrasts. "While he cannot be held entirely free from blame, his youth can be pleaded in extenuation." Here **while** is equivalent to **whereas, though, although**. Care must be taken not to apply **while** in this non-temporal sense to events, circumstances, etc., that are not simultaneous, or absurdities will result. "While a rebellion anywhere called W. H. Nevinson's powers into exercise, a suspension of warring elements allowed his mind to wander freely in poetry and scholarship." The "rebellion" and the "suspension" could not be simultaneous. "While his father and grandfather were educated at Oxford, he went to Cambridge."

whilst is now seldom used.

AUTHENTIC, GENUINE   12

These words can be closely synonymous, but in a distinctive sense **authentic** means that facts given in an account are not fictitious; **genuine**, that a person to whom something is ascribed (e.g. a portrait) is its actual creator, or that something truly belongs to a given period (e.g. a piece of furniture).

authentic is often used today pretentiously in a loose sense of **good, excellent, praiseworthy, sound,** etc. Thus in a review of a novel a contemporary writer is said to have an "authentic" style.

13   I (a) BARBARISM, (b) BARBARITY, (c) BARBAROUSNESS; II (d) BARBARIAN, (e) BARBARIC, (f) BARBAROUS

All these words imply an absence of civilization, or the existence, in what is in general a civilized community, of certain conditions, conduct, etc., associated with an uncivilized society.

I (a)=uncivilized condition. We talk of "relapsing into barbarism".

(b) gross cruelty typical of (a): e.g. the barbarity of some criminal code.

(c)=(a) or (b).

II (d) an adjectival use of the noun **barbarian**=a person living in an uncivilized condition.

(e)=rude, rough: "barbaric splendour".

(f)=uncivilized (in a bad sense), cruel: "barbarous conduct".

barbarism is used also for an outlandish, clumsy, philologically unsound word: e.g. a hybrid (a combination of words or roots from two languages).

14   BASE, BASIS

These words agree in implying something on which something else rests. **base**, however, is generally used with reference to a material thing; **basis**, figuratively. We talk of the **base** of a mountain, a pyramid, a triangle; of the **basis** of an argument, accusation, belief.

commence belongs to the class of what H. W. Fowler in *M.E.U.* calls "formal words": words that are not the common English for what is meant, but translations of them into language that is held more suitable for public exhibition. The less of such translation there is, Fowler urges, the better.

In an earlier book, *The King's English*, H. W. and F. G. Fowler recommend that the familiar word, the short word, and the Saxon word should be preferred to the far-fetched, the long, the Romance. Quiller-Couch in his book *On the Art of Writing* calls in question, as subject to too many exceptions to be a sound guide, the recommendation about the short and the Saxon word. It will generally be found, however, that if one follows the principle, advocated alike by the Fowlers, Quiller-Couch, and Sir Ernest Gowers in *Plain Words*, of choosing the familiar—the common, ordinary, simple, plain—word, the result will nearly always be that one is using a Saxon word and a word shorter than its Romance synonym.

If there is doubt whether a given word should be regarded as a formal one, the only appeal can be to the practice of good contemporary prose writers. The qualifications of "contemporary" and "prose" are important. Language is a living and continually changing thing. Many words used in the past by good writers would not be suitable today; and words used even today in poetry, where choice may be dictated by the needs of rhyme or rhythm, might strike an affected or pompous note in prose.

Often the use of formal words is a sign that speakers or writers wish to be taken as better educated than they really are. Usages prompted by this motive might be called "show-words" of the sham-erudite.

Fowler, in deprecating the use of formal words, adds that he does not recommend that the person thinking in slang should write in slang, or that formal words must always be avoided. Some formal words have special and traditional uses. Thus **proceed**, for **go**, is for ordinary purposes a formal word, but is common in military language, in which a military unit is said to "proceed to a depot " (see 268).

Similarly a play is billed to "commence at 7 o'clock;" military manœuvres "commence in July;" a post is advertised to have a "commencing salary"; and the word has associations with law procedure, divine service, and ceremonial. Otherwise, however, **begin** should be preferred as the natural word, whether in a transitive or intransitive use, and especially when followed by **to**.

If the question is asked why, apart from the consideration that in practice today **begin** is generally used by the best speakers and writers, it ought to be preferred to **commence**, several answers can be given. (1) It is the word that people would naturally use unless they were, however unknowingly, influenced by the popularity of **commence** in newspapers, magazines, and inferior novels and other books. (2) It has honourable associations with the literature of the past. Sir Alan Herbert, in *What a Word*, setting some exercises for his imaginary pupil Bobby, gives six quotations illustrating the use of **begin** and **beginning**—with implied contrast to **commence** and **commencement**—including the first sentence in the Bible ("In the beginning God created the heaven and the earth"), "The lights begin to twinkle from the rocks" (Tennyson's *Ulysses*), and the nursery rhyme, "When the pie was opened the birds began to sing". (3) It is more euphonious. (4) It is shorter: five letters instead of eight. To these four considerations there will be added a fifth by those who, with other things equal, prefer the native Saxon to the Romance Anglo-French word. Journalese, however, has almost banished **begin** from its vocabulary, and so apparently has a large majority of teachers, to judge from their pupils' performances at school examinations for certificates in English language and literature. The same considerations apply to **commencement**.

start: Treble and Vallins in *An ABC of English Usage* say that **start** is best restricted to physical motion: "A train starts at such a time; so does a race". The word, however, shows signs of becoming firmly established for general purposes as not only a substitute for, but a successful rival of, **begin**. Most persons today would probably say "I must start to economize in cigarettes", "I shall start reading the book tomorrow", "The quarrel started over a trifle". Moreover in a context where there may be no implication of physical action **start** can be the more idiomatic. Recently the Court of Appeal in its judgment held that "a man did not cease to be a member of his mother's family on marriage although he might be starting another family of his own". **beginning** here would today be less idiomatic. **start** no doubt owes its popularity partly to its one syllable, partly because its sharp sound has an onomatopoeic effect.

Both **begin** and **start** are used with a special sense of **originate** (**start** is here rather the more idiomatic). "It was this remark that began (or started) the trouble." Another word with this sense is **initiate**. "During the first World War my father initiated the staggering of the staff's holidays." It is sometimes used in journalese[1] as equivalent to **begin** or **start** in their ordinary senses.

What applies to these verbs applies also to the corresponding nouns **beginning, commencement, start. recommence** and **recommencement,** however, are ordinary working words, on a level with **restart** (verb and noun), for neither **begin** nor **beginning** has a corresponding compound word.

The recommendation in *The King's English* about Saxon words is not intended to be an absolute injunction, but to refer only to a preference for Saxon when there exist side by side two or more words that in a given context would be identical in meaning. English owes much of its richness to

---

[1] Journalese is a common and useful word, which, though used here and elsewhere in this book in a depreciatory sense, has no reflection on journalism in general or on journalists, who include today, as they have done in the past, many honoured writers of high rank.

the mixture of Saxon and Romance.[1] Often, especially for abstract ideas, there is no Saxon alternative to the Romance. Moreover to apply the recommendation would sometimes need, as the Fowlers admit, more philological knowledge than most speakers and writers have. They cite eighteen Romance words beginning with b, from the preface of the *Oxford English Dictionary*, of which "few not deep in philology would be prepared to state that no one was English". Nevertheless, especially when synonyms are in question, the Saxon word is generally able to be recognized, even by those with no knowledge of French or Latin, by its form and sound, giving it, as a pro-Saxon enthusiast metaphorically puts it, "a distinctive English tang", e.g. to take a pair of words dealt with in this article, **begin** as compared with **commence**. The articles that follow provide many other examples: e.g. (with the Saxon word placed first) **call, designate; end, terminate, conclude; find, discover; hide, conceal; praise, eulogy; read, peruse; see, perceive, discern; send, dispatch; stop, desist; truthful, veracious; try, endeavour; understand, comprehend.**

16 BENIGNANT, BENIGN, BENEVOLENT, BENEFICENT

To the extent to which any distinction exists **benignant** and **benevolent** refer rather to intention or disposition, and are therefore restricted to persons; **benign** and **beneficent** refer to effect, and are not so restricted. A kind or charitable person is **benignant** or **benevolent**. If his actions have happy

---

[1] Romance in its philological sense refers to words of Latin origin reaching the language at various stages and in various ways. Some have come directly from classical Latin, adapted by writers, or invented, especially during the last hundred years or so, by scientists and technicians. Others have come indirectly from non-classical Latin, mostly through Norman French, which, with other dialects, formed the basis of what are sometimes called the Mediterranean languages—modern French, Spanish, etc. The word Romance is often used also to apply to words from ancient Greek.

results, he is **beneficent**, and if these actions become well-known, or are on a large scale, he may exercise a **benign** influence on his fellow-creatures.

In medical language a harmless growth is a **benign** one, as opposed to a malignant one.

Compare **malignant, malign; malevolent, maleficent** (194).

BEREAVEMENT, LOSS 17

bereavement is a long word and on the formal side (see 15), but, whereas **loss** is a general word, **bereavement** is distinctive in implying that the particular loss referred to is one caused by death.

BLITZ, ATTACK, DAMAGE 18

The noun **blitz**, for **attack** on or for **damage** caused by intense aerial attack, is frowned on by some of those with sufficient knowledge of German to appreciate that **Blitz** means "lightning", and is joined to **Krieg** (="war"), to form the compound word **Blitzkrieg**, i.e. "lightning war", but it seems to have become established. The word is now, however, being extended to cover other sorts of energetic action, even when directed at beneficial purposes. Thus we are told by a statesman that what is needed in the mining industry is to "get a real blitz upon the work".

blitz is used also as a verb, meaning to damage by aerial offence, especially in the past participle, e.g. "blitzed areas".

BLOOM, BLOSSOM, FLOWER 19

flower is the ordinary working word. Fowler says that strictly **bloom** (noun and verb) refers to the **flower** as itself the ultimate achievement of the plant, and blossom (noun and verb) to the **flower** as promising fruit. Thus roses are said to be in **bloom**, apple trees in **blossom**. On the other hand neither **bloom** nor **blossom**, but **flower**, would ordinarily be used for fruiting bushes and small fruiting plants: the gooseberries or strawberries in a garden would be said to be "in flower".

All three nouns have metaphorical uses, especially **flower** and **bloom** (as have also the corresponding nouns): "in the flower of her beauty"; "the bloom of youth".

20   BRITON, BRITISHER

With reference to early history a **Briton** means a member of the Celtic race found by the Romans in the south of England. With reference to people now living a **Briton** is a native of Britain (or Great Britain), i.e. England, Wales, and Scotland—or of the British Empire (or Commonwealth). *C.O.D.* enters the word so used as "poetic, melodramatic, etc.", but, if we are to have a single comprehensive word for this sense, there is no other unless it is to be displaced by **Britisher** (originally an American word), which some dislike.

21   BROTHERS, BRETHREN

brothers is the ordinary form for sons of the same mother. There are, however, figurative phrases like "brothers in arms", "brothers in misfortune".

brethren, the older form, is rarely used now except for fellow members of a religious society, guild, etc.

22   BRUTAL, BRUTISH, BEASTLY, BESTIAL

In some contexts these words would be interchangeable, but distinctions are discernible. **brutal, beastly, bestial** can refer to character or action; **brutish** refers to character. With reference to action **brutal** and **beastly** can apply to what is done or said; **bestial** usually only to what is done.

As most commonly used, **brutal** means coarsely cruel; **brutish** without intelligence or refinement; **beastly**, often colloquial in a trivial sense, nasty, unpleasant ("a **beastly** cold", "a **beastly** day"); **bestial**, violently lustful, depraved.

These meanings of the four adjectives, and the figurative use of the nouns **brute** and **beast**, are based on a conception of the life of animals, compared with that of men—of "nature red in tooth and claw",—as concerned wholly or mostly with the satisfaction of physical needs; lacking reason and intellectual interests; unguided by the moral standards of human beings. Man's attitude, however, to the animal world has in recent times changed considerably from what it used to be, with his increasing observation, study, and realization of the shortcomings in his understanding of it. The use therefore of the words **brutal,** etc., based on too simple an analysis of the life of the **brutes** and the **beasts,** may, in application to what is most vile and degraded in human beings, seem unsuitable to sensitive speakers and writers who will probably prefer to express themselves differently.

BURLESQUE, SKIT, PARODY, CARICATURE, 23 TRAVESTY, LAMPOON

All these words are used for deliberate exaggeration designed to arouse laughter or ridicule. In some contexts the words, used with a general meaning, especially when a private and impromptu taking-off of a person or events is concerned, could be interchanged. In more precise uses the distinctions are as follows.

A **burlesque** consists of action on the stage; a **parody** of writing, speaking, singing; a **caricature** of a drawing of a person's appearance. A **skit** is a colloquial word for a **burlesque** or **parody**. A **travesty** is used for what professes to be a truthful account, but actually gives a glaringly and absurdly false one: "He claims that the recent account by Mr. Molotov of what was happening in Palestine was a complete travesty of the facts". A **lampoon** is a virulent satire (see 168).

In the sense of setting forth in words the characteristics of a person or thing **call**, **describe** (as), and **term** are the working words: e.g. "He called this sheer robbery". **designate**, **denominate** and **style** are show-words (see 15).

25 CAPACITY, ABILITY, CAPABILITY, APTITUDE

In some contexts the words would be interchangeable. As far as differences in meaning are recognizable, **ability** refers rather to faculties of which a person has shown proof ("I was much impressed by the **ability** with which he dealt with this delicate matter"); **capability**, generally used in the plural, and **capacity** to the potential exercise of faculties ("I think my new secretary has great capabilities;" "She has a remarkable capacity for learning languages").

ability and **capability** (capabilities) are generally used absolutely; **capacity** with reference to a particular mentioned talent, etc. (as in the examples just given). **aptitude** is closer in sense to **capacity** than to the two other words, as meaning potential talent with reference to a particular activity.

26   CATEGORY, CLASS, DIVISION

category is properly a specialized philosophical word, the **categories** of philosophy being the fundamental **classes** to which human knowledge can be reduced, e.g. substance, quantity, quality, place, time. The word is often used by the sham-erudite (see 15) as merely a substitute for **class** or **division.**

27   CEILING, LIMIT

ceiling was formerly used only literally for the roof of a room. It has recently become a vogue-word (see 34) in a metaphorical sense for an extreme limit attainable or allowable in human action. It is used especially with reference to a numerical **limit**: e.g. in the maximum height an aeroplane can be taken, or in the production of goods. "Unless the Far Eastern Commission establishes new ceilings Japanese peaceful industries will be allowed unrestricted development after October 1st." "The badly nourished child may never grow up to the ceiling of physical stature inheritable from his parents." In a special use it is sometimes said, of a task so easy as to give a person little scope for showing his true ability, that "it has no ceiling".

CEREMONIAL, CEREMONIOUS 28

Both words mean "formal". **ceremonial** is applied to procedure, especially in matters of church or state or law: e.g. a ceremonial entry of soldiers into a captured city, the ceremonial installation of the Lord Mayor of London, the ceremonial costume in which he was dressed. **ceremonious** is applied to persons and to behaviour. "My host was distant and ceremonious." Such a host in saying good-bye might give a ceremonious bow instead of shaking hands.

CHANGE, ALTER 29

In many contexts these two words are interchangeable. There is, however, even among those who would usually prefer a Saxon and short word to a Romance and longer one, a preference for **alter**. This is probably because **change** has so many other meanings, especially with the sense of exchange: e.g. "change one's clothes", "change trains", "change places" with a person. *C.O.D.* has five lines for **alter**, 21 for **change**. In such circumstances there is in language a natural tendency, so as to avoid ambiguity or false scent, to prefer the word with only one or a few meanings to that with many. Compare **difficult** (71), **endeavour** (89), **expensive** (101), **impecunious** (149), **wealthy** (311).

cheerful refers rather to the disposition of a person; **cheery** to his manner. A **cheerful** person might not show positive signs of being so, and so might not be called **cheery;** and a **cheery** person, though in his manner showing signs that indicated his being **cheerful**, might not in his heart be so.

31   CHILDLIKE, CHILDISH

childlike refers to good qualities, when shown by adults, that are associated with children: e.g. simplicity, innocence, candour.

> God gives thee youth but once: keep thou
> The childlike heart that would His kingdom be.

childish is used (*a*) in a derogatory sense with reference to unadmirable qualities shown by adults: e.g. peevishness, which might be excusable in children (compare **puerile**, 400); (*b*) with reference to a person in second-childhood, dotage.

32   CLASSICAL, CLASSIC

In their strictest use **classical** refers to Latin and Greek writers, art, culture; **classic** means "of the highest class." Thus Virgil is a "classical writer;" the Parthenon at Athens is "classical architecture;" and we have the idioms "classical quotations," "classical features;" but the Derby is a "classic race."

33   CLIENT, CUSTOMER

A **client** is a person in his relation to members of certain professions, for whose services he pays: e.g. a solicitor, an architect, a banker. (This does not apply to all professional people to whom fees are paid: e.g. a doctor has a **patient**; a teacher, a **pupil**.) A **customer** is a person in his relation, as a buyer, to a person or firm engaged in trade.

colourful is not only used with deadening frequency as an epithet for any material scene that literally has colour, but also, as a substitute for **vivid, interesting**, etc., it is applied to abstract things: e.g. a person's character, an incident, a story; and is used in even more remote applications: thus *The Times*, in an article on a new French government, referred to M. Blum's "colourful experiments" in economics.

colourful belongs to a class of words springing into popularity that are called by Fowler "vogue-words". They may be new words or they may introduce a new use of an old word. Sometimes a cause of their being taken up is that at first they have the charm of novelty. At a later stage, when they have come into common usage, they are seized upon by people too lazy to select a word more suitable for the context. Naturally writers or speakers of individuality and vigour will use them as little as possible. Often still later the use of such words is extended; their original sense becomes blurred; they are given meanings that they cannot properly bear, or are used in so slipshod a way that it is not clear what the speaker or writer even intends them to mean in a given context.

colour as noun and verb has metaphorical meanings: e.g. "The discovery lends some colour to the charges"; "His criticisms are clearly coloured by animus". This use of the noun has not escaped extension, like that of **colourful**, to cloudy effects. Sir Herbert Grierson (in *Rhetoric and English Composition*), with one comprehensive daub, puts it forward as a useful noun to cover "the associations which gather round a word by long usage; accidental circumstances connected with our experience of the word—the people who used it, the places in which we have heard it, the other words and ideas that it tends to excite".

35 COMMONPLACE, PLATITUDE, TRUISM, AXIOM

A **commonplace** is something often said; an everyday, common, saying. It is therefore destitute of originality. It may be true or false. If true, the statement may or may not be of value. A **platitude** is a statement of something, as if it were important, that does not need stating; a trite remark. It is therefore never of value. A **truism** in its strict, but seldom used, sense is a statement that repeats what is already implicit, or a statement too hackneyed to be worth making. Thus "To act with too great haste is unwise" is a **truism** because the sense of "is unwise" is already contained in the statement that the "haste" is "too great". In a slipshod way **truism** is used to mean a statement that is indisputably true, and therefore needs no proof, and cannot be contradicted. The correct word for this meaning would be **axiom**, which means a "self-evident truth".

36 COMPARATIVELY, RELATIVELY, RATHER, SOMEWHAT

comparatively and **relatively** ought to refer to something that has been mentioned explicitly or is implied, but the words are often used in a loose way where there is no standard of comparison, as an equivalent of **rather, somewhat, fairly**, etc. "We enjoyed comparatively fine weather during our holiday": compared with what? The weather that might have been expected then? That people in other districts had? That we had last year? Similarly, in a loose and indeterminate use of the adjective: "They live in comparative luxury (or poverty)"; "She had a relatively uneventful life". (This use of **relatively** is perhaps more excusable than of **comparatively** because it may be regarded as having an implied opposition to **absolutely**.)

hide is the ordinary working word. It is used both with reference to concrete things and figuratively. One **hides** a bank note in a book, and one **hides** one's feelings. **conceal**- also is used in both ways, but is slightly on the formal side except in a figurative sense. **secrete** is generally restricted to concrete things.

Though the verb **conceal** is on the formal side, the noun **concealment** is an ordinary working word, more common than **hiding**.

CONCEPTION, CONCEPT, IDEA 38

Whatever is before the mind when one thinks may be described as an **idea** or **ideas**. The process of forming **ideas** does not call for much thought. We readily form the **idea** of a chair, a triangle, an explosion. If, however, intellectual effort is needed for the abstraction of a quality from its embodiment in material things: e.g. of whiteness, or solubility, or gravity, we speak of an **idea** of this class as a **concept**. Thus "Einstein gave us the concept of relativity".

The general process of forming abstract **ideas** is some- times called **conception**, but such **ideas** themselves have in the past been usually called **conceptions**, especially when they have been formed by the combination of ideas ("A poet with great powers of conception").

CONCOURSE, CROWD 39

concourse is a formal word (see 15) for an assembly of people (or things) drawn together. **crowd** is a more homely word for people closely pressed together.

CONFIRM, VERIFY, CHECK, CHECK UP, 40
CHECK UP ON, CORROBORATE, ENDORSE

The general idea common to these words is of making certain, establishing as true or correct, something spoken or written.

confirm is the ordinary working word, but it is used also, as the other words are not, in the sense of establishing more firmly the power or possession of a person: e.g. with reference to an appointment that is **confirmed** by a higher authority.

check is on the colloquial side.

In **check up, check up on,** and—less common here than in U.S.A.—**check on,** the adverbial particles **up, up on, on,** do not add anything to the sense of the bare verb, and are therefore mere verbosity. Compare **face up to** (106) and **manned up** (196).

verify is generally used with reference to a figure, date, or quotation.

corroborate is restricted to **confirming** a statement, or giving support to its maker, by personal evidence.

endorse, which is more commonly used for signing one's name on the back of a cheque or other document, or for accepting formally an arrangement, is used also for supporting the expressed opinion of a person: e.g. we **endorse** (or we do not **endorse**) the policy of the Government; when a motorist's or a publican's licence is **endorsed** a record of the proved offence is written on the back of it.

41   CONSERVATIVE, MODERATE, CAUTIOUS

conservative in its primary sense means "preservative", "that which preserves". Thence it became applied to opinions in favour of preserving existing institutions, or to persons holding these opinions, especially the English Conservative Party. In a further extension, which Fowler 22 years ago deplored as slipshod, it has become established as an epithet for figures in estimates, etc., meaning **moderate, cautious,** "less than one might reasonably have conjectured". "The report of the Churches' Committee gives £650 million spent in 1948 on gambling as a conservative estimate."

The verb **contact** is not yet recognized by *C.O.D.* In the *Shorter Oxford English Dictionary* it is entered as "rare, technical". In its journalesey use to-day with the sense of **meet** it is an unnecessary word. "As we advanced we contacted a crowd of panic-stricken refugees fleeing from their homes." It is often used, however, for "get into touch with" a person, which one can do without meeting him. "After tiresome delay he succeeded in contacting the secretary of the American branch of the company." "For applying for an export licence he had known which department of the Board of Trade to contact." Its convenience for expressing in one word what otherwise needs four will probably cause it to become established. Sir Ernest Gowers in *Plain Words* seems resigned to the usage.

The verb is sometimes found also in an intransitive use. "We arranged to contact again as soon as possible."

There have been two recent extensions of the noun **contact**. One is in its use for the person with whom **contact** is made: e.g. "I knew about this from information given me by one of our contacts, who was in the high counsels of the Nazis". The other is an adjectival use. Thus there is the term "contact man", and a firm with the name of Contact Publications Limited publish a series called "The Contact Books".

CONTAGIOUS, INFECTIOUS 43

In the medical sense a disease spread by touch (Latin *tango*="touch") is said to be **contagious**; if otherwise, **infectious**. Metaphorically, not restricted to a bad sense (e.g. gaiety as well as fear can be **infectious**), the two words are identical in meaning.

Consider a parcel in which are packed three articles: A, B, C. The parcel **contains** A, B, C. If, however, one wishes to confine one's reference to only one or two of them— e.g. A and B—it is safer for the avoidance of ambiguity to say the parcel **includes** A and B. In ordinary usage a synonym for **contains** in the example given above could be **comprise** or **consist** of. Strictly the parcel is made up of a box, paper, string, etc., as well as of A, B, C.: consequently strictly it is the contents of the parcel that **comprise** or **consist** of A, B, C.

consist in, as distinct from **consist of**, suggests inherent qualities. "The essence of discipline consists in prompt and unquestioning obedience."

45   CONTEMPLATE, MEDITATE, PREMEDITATE

In a synonymous sense these three words have the common idea of "think of doing something". There is a distinction between them in the degree of intention they imply. Thus "I contemplate going to Switzerland for my next holiday" implies that I have reached a point nearer decision than if **meditate** had been used. Moreover one can **meditate** or **contemplate** doing something, and eventually decide against, or be prevented from, doing it. but **premeditate** can hardly be used except with reference to something that did happen. "No doubt at an early stage Hitler premeditated attacking Poland if she did not accept his demands." In a trial for homicide a verdict of manslaughter or of murder may depend on the jury's opinion whether the prisoner's act was **premeditated**.

Both **contemplate** and **meditate** have also the meaning of "be engaged in deep reflection". **contemplate** has two further meanings: (1) "gaze upon", "look at" with the physical eyes or figuratively with the mind; (2) make in the mind an image of something that will or may happen. For this last sense see 389.

[34]

constantly=often. "He is constantly going over to France on business."

continually=at short intervals. "He is continually in trouble at school."

continuously—with no break, without interruption. "That tap was dripping continuously through the night."

perpetually strictly=**eternally**, for ever, but is mostly used colloquially as equivalent to **continually**, as above: generally in a bad sense. "He is perpetually bothering his friends with requests for loans."

incessantly=without ceasing, and therefore strictly=**continuously**, as above, but often used loosely=**continually.**

All the words except **continuously** are restricted to time, but **continuously** and its adjective **continuous** (see next article) can refer also to space. A river can flow **continuously** along the frontier of a state.

In some contexts **continuance** and **continuation** could be interchanged. *M.E.U.* points out that such distinctions as can be recognized are due to the fact that **continuance** is connected with the intransitive use of the verb "continue" ="go on", "last"; **continuation,** with its transitive use= "go on with", and its passive use="be gone on with". So "The continuance of this drought will ruin the harvest" (i.e. not its continuation: the drought is thought of as "going on", and not "gone on with"). On the other hand "I look forward to the continuation of his broadcast next week" (not its continuance: the broadcast is thought of as "gone on with" by the broadcaster, rather than as "going on").

continuity and (rare) **continuousness** mean, with reference to material things, a state of being connected, unbroken;

figuratively, a state of being uninterrupted in time or sequence.

The adjectives **continual** and **continuous** are sometimes synonymous. *C.O.D.* defines **continual** as "always going on" or "very frequent". Treble and Vallins in *An ABC of English Usage* say that in **continual** there is usually the suggestion of intermittency. See also last article.

48   CONTRACT, CATCH, GET

One can, without incurring the charge of using a show-word (see 15), **contract** a habit or a debt, but only journalese and its cousin gentility (see 85) speak of **contracting**, instead of **catching** or **getting**, a cold, measles, etc., or using some phrase like "suffer from", "fall ill with", as for instance in a recent biography of Joseph Goebbels, who, the reader is told, "contracted a boil".

49   CONTROVERSIAL, CONTENTIOUS

In the sense of "open to argument", as in Sir Roger de Coverley's statement that "much might be said on both sides", the words might be interchanged. **contentious,** but not **controversial,** can be applied to a person, as well as to a subject of discussion, meaning argumentative.

50   CORPSE, CARCASE

corpse is the dead body of a human being. **carcase** is generally restricted to the dead body of a quadruped of some size.

51   COUNTERPART, DUPLICATE

counterpart in its primary meaning is synonymous with **duplicate,** for one of two things exactly alike. **duplicate** is restricted to things; **counterpart** can refer also in a secondary meaning to people, especially to a person who forms a complement, or is similarly placed, to another. **counterpart** is being displaced today by the clumsy vogue-term (see 34) **opposite number**, especially for a person occupying an official position corresponding to that occupied by another.

CREDIT, CREDENCE   52

In some contexts the two words, in the sense of "belief," are interchangeable. "I do not give much credence to his story," and "I do not give much credit to his story" mean the same, and are equally idiomatic. **credence**, however, has the advantage that it means one thing only, whereas **credit** has several other meanings. A shop gives a person **credit** when, from belief that the customer will pay, it allows him to run up an account. The sum in a bank at a customer's disposal is his **credit**. It means also "acknowledgment of merit" ("He got much credit for the skill with which he handled the affair"), and "source of honour" ("He is a credit to his school").

(1) CRIME, (2) IMMORALITY, (3) VICE,   53
(4) MISDEMEANOUR, (5) FELONY, (6) SIN,
(7) WICKEDNESS, (8) EVIL, (9) NAUGHTINESS,
(10) BADNESS, (11) DELINQUENCY

(1) to (5) can be used with general reference to wrong conduct, or with particular reference to an instance of such conduct.

crime is technically an act that at law counts as a **felony** or **misdemeanour**, but the word is often used loosely for any act that is gravely wrong.

immorality is the violation of the recognized code of morals. It is often used in a narrow sense for sexual misbehaviour.

The *Shorter Oxford English Dictionary* defines **vice** as "moral fault or defect (without implication of serious wrongdoing); a flaw in character or conduct". To some persons, however, a particular **vice** might be more repulsive and seem more serious than a particular **crime**. Moreover there are forms of **vice** that are punishable as **crimes**.

Of indictable offences under the law a **misdemeanour** is less legally grave than a **felony**.

The code according to which certain conduct is regarded in a community as **criminal, immoral, vicious,** a **misdemeanour**, a **felony**, a **sin**, is dependent on the views of the majority of people living at the time. A code may vary from country to country and from age to age. The word **evil**, however, is often used to mean fundamental, absolute, immutable badness. Neville Chamberlain, in his speech in 1939 saying that war had been declared on Germany, described us as fighting against "evil things".

The use of the words **sin** and **wickedness**, which cover **crime, immorality** and **vice**, generally imply today in the user a view towards wrongdoing that regards it in a religious light as an offence against divine law.

badness is seldom used with reference to wrong conduct (for other meanings see dictionary), and then only in a general sense: e.g. "There is no real badness in the boy".

naughtiness and its adjective **naughty** are generally used today either (*a*) facetiously, or (*b*) to or by children, with reference to bad behaviour. Compare (*b*) with the restriction of **scold** (see 55).

delinquency is used today chiefly in the phrase **juvenile delinquency**, as a euphemism for **juvenile crime**: criminal conduct by young offenders—**juvenile delinquents**—whom the law is concerned primarily to reform rather than to punish.

A "venial sin" (Latin *venia*=pardon) implies pardonable, excusable misconduct.

For the ordinary and established meanings of **appreciation** and **evaluation** see dictionary. As vogue-words (see 34) **appreciation, evaluation** and **appraisal** are affected synonyms of **criticism** in the sense of discussion, in an analytical way, with reference to literature and the arts. **appreciation** is generally used (though not necessarily: see below) for a judgment that on the whole is favourable. In a neutral sense it is common today in military language for an opinion of a situation, or of a strategical plan proposed by a superior authority. "In view of arrival of German armoured formations . . . the question of defence commitments in Egypt has been considered here. Would be glad if you would telegraph a short appreciation" (Mr. Winston Churchill to General Wavell). **appraisal**, on account of its derivation from **praise**, is often used incorrectly as a synonym of that word. It can cover, like the other words in this group, an opinion that is unfavourable as well as favourable or a mixture of both. A less common word is **critique**. This is used for an analytical estimate, especially with reference to literature or acted drama, that deals, not as **criticism** and the other words can do, with the work in general of a writer or playwright, but with a single book or play.

criticism, evaluation, and **appraisal** have verbs (**criticize, evaluate, appraise**) used in the same sense, but not **appreciate**.

For **criticism** in a general reference, not applied to literature and the arts, see next article.

(1) CRITICIZE, (2) CONDEMN, (3) BLAME,   55
(4) CENSURE, (5) REPROVE, (6) REBUKE,
(7) REPRIMAND, (8) UPBRAID, (9) REPROACH,
(10) SCOLD, (11) CHIDE

These words in their roughly synonymous sense mean "find fault with".

There are certain general distinctions as follows:

(1) to (4) can have as their object a person or a thing done by a person. (5) to (11) can have only the former.

With (1) to (3) the "finding fault" may be expressed in spoken or written words, or it may remain in the mind unexpressed. The other words (4) to (11) imply expression in words.

(5) to (7), (10), and (11) generally imply the ascription of fault by a superior to a subordinate: (10)—now becoming rare—and (11) for offences not grave.

(8) implies complaint that is expressed bitterly, violently.

For the use of **criticize** and **criticism** that does not imply "finding fault" see last article.

56   CRY, WEEP, SOB, WAIL

The following table shows the main differences when they are observable.

With tears	cry	weep	sob	—
From grief	cry	weep	sob	wail
From pain or rage	cry	—	—	—
From joy	cry	weep	—	—
From fear	cry	—	—	—
From exhaustion	—	—	sob	—

cry is the ordinary working word. **weep** generally implies a quieter utterance than the other words; **sob**, convulsive gasps; **wail**, a loud shrill utterance. **weep** is often used to emphasize an intense note of grief. "Rachel weeping for her children, and would not be comforted, because they were not" (St. Matthew, ii, 18). Shakespeare brings out this contrast between **cry** and **weep** in Antony's funeral speech in *Julius Caesar*: "When that the poor have cried, Caesar hath wept".

cryptic (Greek *krupto*="hide") is (*a*) a show-word (see 15) for **mysterious**; (*b*) a word, beloved by writers of thrillers, for something said that is intended to puzzle or have a hidden meaning.

DEDUCE, INFER, GATHER, UNDERSTAND 58

All these words have the meaning of "reach a conclusion based on previous knowledge". **infer** is the ordinary working word. **deduce** is generally used for a conclusion reached in the course of a scientific or philosophical inquiry, and drawn from the general to the particular. **gather** and **understand** are somewhat colloquial.

For **infer** see also 152; for **understand**, 375.

DEFICIENT, DEFECTIVE 59

Both words imply the lack of something. In many contexts **deficient** refers to a quantitative, **defective** to a qualitative, lack. "The flow of water is deficient"; "That tap is defective". Some lacks, however, may be thought of both quantitatively and qualitatively. Either word is then applicable. Thus a writer can be **deficient** or **defective** in imagination, and a food may be **deficient** or **defective** in vitamins.

A special idiomatic use is shown when in dealing with handicapped children educationists distinguish between the "physically defective" and the "mentally deficient".

An exceptional use is that of the grammatical term "defective verb," for the lack there (i.e. of the normal inflections) is quantitative.

DEFINITE, DEFINITIVE 60

C.O.D. defines **definite** as "with exact limits; determinate, distinct, precise, not vague". **definitive** means "final", "decisive," "unconditional". A **definite** offer is one of which the terms are precise; a **definitive** offer is one of which the terms are not subject to modification.

definite is perhaps today the most common vogue-word (see 34) in the language. Only rarely does one come across a sentence in which it has some meaning. "It had been arranged that he should retire that year. A definite date was now settled, for September 30th." As mostly used, however, it adds nothing to the sense. "This latest move means definite possibilities of a breakdown in the negotiations." The Report of the Chief Medical Officer of the Ministry of Health states that in the weight of school children there was for the year "a slight but definite decline". What sort of a decline would an **indefinite** one be? A judge said some time ago that it would be a good thing if the word were expelled from the language.

61   DEFINITELY, CERTAINLY, UNDOUBTEDLY, SURELY

certainly means "without any doubt," whereas **surely** may convey the suggestion that there is a slight shadow of doubt. "He will certainly accept the offer" implies stronger belief than "He will surely accept it". Indeed **surely** may imply uncertainty rather than certainty, or even a question: "Surely you will not go out in this weather", and in that sense is often followed in writing or print by a mark of interrogation.

definitely, like **definite** (see last article) a vogue-word (see 35), is sometimes equivalent in sense to **certainly**. "The goods will definitely be sent to you this week." Often it is used merely to add emphasis. "I must definitely refuse." More often still it adds nothing to the sense. (1) "The strike has definitely ended." (2) A: "Will you be able to get the work finished this week?" B: "Definitely not." (3) Evidence by a doctor at a coroner's inquest: "I could see that, given the chance, he would definitely commit suicide".

(4) "The makers of the film had to take into account the tastes of audiences that would definitely not be satisfied with a heroine that was ugly." Perhaps the height of absurdity was reached when recently the writer of an article in a newspaper, on a bill that was before Parliament, said that a particular clause was "definitely obscure".

A common colloquial use today of **definitely** is for "Yes" replacing a similar previous use of "Quite". (A) "Are you accepting the invitation?" (B) "Definitely", or even "Absolutely definitely". The adverb might without loss to the language join the adjective in its expulsion (see last article, 60).

DELIGHTFUL, DELICIOUS, DELECTABLE 62

delightful is a general word for that which gives great pleasure: a "delightful companion", a "delightful evening". **delicious** is restricted to the pleasures of taste and smell, or is used colloquially with reference to a humorous incident or story, or to a joke, which metaphorically one may regard as savouring on one's tongue; and a person is said to have a "delicious sense of humour".

delectable is a poetic synonym of **delightful**. Bunyan wrote "They came to the Delectable Mountains".

DENY, REPUDIATE 63

In their synonymous relation, with reference to an accusation, meaning "declare to be false", **repudiate** implies that the declaration is made with strong feeling, especially of indignation.

DEPRECIATE, DISPARAGE, DECRY, 64 DENIGRATE, DEBUNK

The common idea in the words is "belittle the value of", "show one's low opinion of". **depreciate, disparage,** and

decry can refer to a person or his character, reputation, work, etc.; **denigrate** and **debunk** only to a person. **decry** is generally used for belittling publicity. **denigrate** (Latin *niger*=black) would have been regarded a few years ago as a somewhat pretentious word but is now common. It is used especially for attempting to undermine established reputations, as for example by Lytton Strachey in *Eminent Victorians*. **debunk** (of American origin) is a recent and rough word for this.

65   DEPRESSION, DEJECTION, DESPONDENCY, MELANCHOLY

These four words imply an unhappy state of mind. **melancholy** generally implies a temperamental tendency to gloomy thoughts, though not necessarily showing itself in a gloomy demeanour. There is the proverbial jester with quips and smiling face but a heavy heart. **despondency**, **dejection, depression**, refer to a state of downheartedness, generally showing themselves in a person's outward bearing. These three words are derived from Latin. **despondency** (*despondere*="to give up") and **dejection** (*dejectus*="cast down") usually revolve round a particular cause for happiness; **depression** (*depressus*="pressed down") is often more general, and perhaps comes and goes: we speak of "fits of depression".

66   DERIVE, ORIGINATE, STEM

The common established use of **derive** is as a transitive verb. "Shakespeare derived the main plot of *Macbeth* from Holinshed's *Chronicles*." "Many Romance words are derived, not directly from Latin, but through French." Today the word is coming into frequent use (Sir Ernest Gowers in *Plain Words* gives it among a number of words that are "overworked"), intransitively="have its derivation from", as a synonym of **originate, spring, come.** "The character of Mr. Rose in Mallock's *New Republic* is said to have derived from that of Walter Pater." "The lack of emotion in Swift's sermons seems to derive from a deeper cause." "The rights of the United Kingdom in Berlin derive from the unconditional surrender of Germany." The *Shorter Oxford English Dictionary* gives this usage as going back to Middle English; for modern times it cites Mark Pattison (died 1884): "Puritanism derives to this country from Geneva".

Journalese is trying to introduce as another synonym of **originate** the verb **stem.** It is given in the *Shorter Oxford English Dictionary* as coming from U.S.A. "His powers stemmed from the will rather than the imagination."

DESIGNATION, DESCRIPTION, TERM, 67
NAME, TITLE

designation is a show-word (see 15) for **description** and the three other words.

DETERIORATE, WORSEN, DEGENERATE 68

All three words can imply that what was good becomes bad, or what was bad becomes worse.

deteriorate (Latin *deterior*="worse"), though given in the dictionaries as having a rare transitive use ("make worse"), is generally used only intransitively ("become worse", "change for the worse"). Perhaps that is why this long and clumsy Romance word (how often we hear it pronounced "deteriate"!) is often unconsciously chosen in preference to the short and simple Saxon **worsen,** which is commonly used both intransitively and transitively.

The verb **degenerate** has the distinctive meaning that the condition of becoming worse involves a loss of some quality proper to the person or thing that has undergone change.

"After we had been climbing for a couple of hours the weather deteriorated", but "What had begun as an orderly and amicable discussion degenerated into a vulgar squabble", and "In later years the character of Bonnie Prince Charlie, from its brilliance and charm in youth, sadly degenerated".

69   DIFFERENCE, DIFFERENTIATION

The **difference** between two things is the quality, quantity, etc., with reference to which they are not the same. **differentiation** is (*a*) the formulation of a difference, a distinction, between things, or (*b*) an operation of putting this into effect. (*a*) "He explained that he was not a strict vegetarian, and that he made a differentiation between eating a wild creature like a grouse, which one went out to kill for sport, and a barndoor fowl, which owed its existence, feeding, and protection to man." (*b*) "Communism postulates equality, but the Soviet system shows a considerable differentiation between the citizens in awarding privileges to certain classes of workers."

70   DIFFERENT, DIVERSE

In some contexts these words could be interchanged, but **diverse** generally implies a wider or sharper contrast than **different**. "Diverse opinions were expressed" implies more of a clash than if **different** were used.

71   DIFFICULT, HARD

The two words, in the sense of "not easy," are closely synonymous. It might be expected that, except at all events by the tribe of speakers and writers enamoured of long words, the shorter Saxon **hard** would be more commonly used than its longer Romance alternative, but this is not so. **hard**, unlike **difficult**, has many meanings. Thus in a recent speech the two words appeared in the same sentence with different meanings: "Our present hard privations can be cured only by the difficult though not impossible task of increased production". *C.O.D.* gives 60 lines to the uses of **hard**; four to **difficult**. This probably explains why, in accordance with a principle mentioned before, there is a tendency to prefer **difficult** to **hard**. Compare the uses of **alter** (29), **endeavour** (89), **expensive** (101), **impecunious** (149), **wealthy** (311). Moreover **difficult** is an adjective connected with the familiar noun **difficulty**, used in the same sense, of what is opposite to **easy**, whereas **hard** has for its noun **hardness**, which is not so commonly used in that sense. We would speak rather of the **difficulty** than of the **hardness** of a problem. Perhaps also it is not too fanciful to imagine that the very length of **difficult**, compared with **hard**, and its not being so easy to pronounce, give it an onomatopoeic, a "sense from sound", value. Compare **endeavour** (89), **numerous** (197), **permission** (241), **consequence** (303).

DIFFICULTY, QUANDARY, DILEMMA   72

difficulty is the general word, and covers the two others.

A **quandary** and a **dilemma** are particular types of **difficulty** in which a person does not know what to do. To be in a **quandary** means that it is necessary to take some step, but that one is puzzled what that step shall be. To be in, or on the horns of, a **dilemma** means to be in a situation where the only choice of action is between two evils, or to be engaged in an argument in which a person is forced to choose one of two alternatives both unwelcome to him. In a colloquial phrase, "he is in a fix".

DISAPPROVE, DEPRECATE   73

The primary meaning of **deprecate** is "plead against". To "deprecate a person's anger" is to "beseech him not to be angry". In a secondary meaning of "have a wish against," "have an unfavourable opinion of", **deprecate** is roughly synonymous with **disapprove**. Distinctions between the two words are as follows. (1) **disapprove** can refer both to persons and things; **deprecate** only to things. (2) **disapprove** can refer to an opinion that is expressed, or to one that remains in the mind unexpressed; **deprecate** only to the former. (3) **disapprove** generally implies a higher degree of unfavourable opinion than **deprecate**.

74   DISCOVER, FIND, FIND OUT, ASCERTAIN

In many contexts these words could be interchanged: "I found (or discovered) a stray cat in the shed"; "She found (or discovered) that the whole story was a lie". **find**, however, is the working word, especially with reference to something that one comes across, lights upon, by accident, whereas, if this occurs in the course of search or inquiry, **discover** (French *découvrir*="to uncover") is the more usual word, especially with reference to something in the sphere of science or exploration that has not been known before. "Primitive man discovered how to make fire." "Harvey discovered the circulation of the blood." "Galileo discovered that the earth moves round the sun." "Speke discovered the sources of the Nile." **ascertain** is a show-word (see 15), restricted to the figurative sense of **discover**, **find**, especially when followed by a noun ("that") clause. **find out** is colloquial for **discover, find,** in this sense.

75   DISINTERESTED, UNINTERESTED, IMPARTIAL,
UNBIASED

As the prefixes un- and dis- signify "not", **uninterested** and **disinterested** both mean in a general way "not interested", "without interest", but they have distinct implications, though they are often used as if they were exact synonyms.

The words correspond respectively to two different senses of the noun "interest". This can mean (*a*) curiosity, concern; (*b*) pecuniary or other stake, advantage, etc. **uninterested** is related to (*a*); **disinterested** to (*b*).

uninterested: if A says that as a boy he did not care for tales of adventure, and took no interest in *Treasure Island*, he was **uninterested**, but not **disinterested**, in the book.

disinterested: X and Y are in disagreement about a certain transaction in which X claims that Y owes him money. Z is called in to arbitrate. Z has no pecuniary interest in the matter and does not even know X and Y personally. He is indifferent which of them is in the right; is **impartial**; **unbiased**; **disinterested**. This is not to say that he is **uninterested**. On the contrary he may find the arguments on the two sides, and the rights and wrongs of the case, highly interesting. (See also p. 198.)

There is not a noun corresponding to **uninterested**. Consequently **disinterestedness** has to serve both for a state of being **uninterested** and for being **disinterested**, and the precise meaning can be gauged only from the context.

It is to be noted as a general principle that, though we are told that "two negatives make a positive", the implication of a double negative is generally weaker than that of the single affirmative. Thus a meal that was served up "not hot" might not be "cold" but "lukewarm." To be **not uninterested** in anything is a milder form of concern than to be **interested** in it.

The verb **disinterest** is generally used reflexively. "To disinterest oneself" is "to cease to concern oneself", especially in diplomacy; "to renounce the intention or right of intervening" (*C.O.D.*).

DISPOSAL, DISPOSITION   76

M.E.U. points out that **disposition** corresponds to the verb "dispose", and **disposal** to the verb "dispose of". So a **disposition** of troops refers to their station for action; their

disposal to the way in which they are lodged, etc. Some-times, however, the two conditions are only a description of the same act from a different point of view, and the words can then be used indiscriminately: e.g. of the **disposition** or the **disposal** of property by will.

77   DISTINCT, DISTINCTIVE

distinct means "well-marked", "clearly defined", and so "easily discernible". A speaker's enunciation can be **distinct**; so can a Scottish accent; and a person can be given a "distinct snub". Often, however, the word is used as not much more than an emphasizer: "The play last night was a distinct success".

distinctive means "marking or expressing difference", "serving as a token by which something may be known from others of its kind". We may refer e.g. to the **distinctive** watermarks of postage stamps, the **distinctive** colour-marks on birds' eggs; at a public meeting stewards wear **distinctive** badges; doctors diagnose various types of fever by a **distinctive** rash.

78   DIVIDEND, PROFIT, ADVANTAGE

A **dividend** (apart from its mathematical sense, for a number to be divided by a divisor) is a sum of money pay-able out of profit to the shareholders or creditors of a joint stock company, or as interest on a loan. In recent years it has become a vogue-word (see 34) with reference to a course of action that produces satisfactory results unconnected with financial operations, i.e. as a substitute for (non-monetary) **profit, advantage.** "Amateur photography is a hobby that with a little patience and attention to simple rules will easily produce dividends." "This general was allowed to have a different organization from that of other divisions. He had a tank component and more guns. This complicated some of the staff work, but it paid a handsome dividend." How weary one becomes of that phrase!

stray is used both in a physical sense, for wandering from or losing the path or the right direction, and figuratively: e.g. for losing the path of virtue, or in speaking and writing for leaving the main topic (e.g. "stray from the point").

digress and **divagate** are generally restricted to this figurative use with reference to speaking and writing.

DOCTOR, PHYSICIAN, SURGEON   80

doctor is mostly used in a general way for any member of the medical profession. He treats patients medically, and should be addressed as **Doctor** (Dr.), whether he holds the degree of Doctor of Medicine or not. **physician** is the more formal word applied to a **doctor** in a position higher than that of general practitioner. A **surgeon** is a member of the medical profession who treats diseases by operation, and, whether holding a doctor's degree or not, should be addressed as Mr. or Mrs. or Miss.

The holder of the highest university degree in any faculty, whether medicine, science, music, whether honorary or not, is a **doctor** in that faculty and should be so addressed.

DOFF, TAKE OFF; DON, PUT ON   81

A form of affectation by journalese is to substitute an archaic for an ordinary current word. Among such archaisms—"antiquarian rubbish, Wardour-Street English", *M.E.U.* calls them—are **doff** and **don** (by derivation "do off", "do on"), for **take off** and **put on** clothes.

DRESS, FROCK, ROBE, GOWN, COSTUME   82

dress is the working word. **frock** is colloquial for **dress** for an adult, or in general use it refers to the **dress** of a child. **robe** is an outer garment worn for a ceremonial occasion: e.g. "christening robe", "coronation robes". **gown**, except when it refers to the ceremonial garment worn by a graduate, is a trade word for a **dress** on sale. **costume** is another word

for a dress on sale, or a colloquialism for a coat and skirt
for day wear, but it is also used in a generic sense for "style
of dressing": e.g. "man's costume in the Elizabethan age".

83   DRUNK, DRUNKEN, INTOXICATED
                INEBRIATED, TIPSY

   drunk is used as a predicative adjective: "That man is
drunk;" **drunken** as an attributive adjective: "The drunken
woman lurched towards me". **intoxicated** and **inebriated** are
formal words (see 15).
   drunk and **intoxicated** are used also metaphorically, to
mean "excited", "exalted": e.g. "drunk with joy", "I grew
intoxicated with my own eloquence" (in *Contarini Fleming*,
by Disraeli, who earlier facetiously spoke of Gladstone as
"inebriated with the exuberance of his own verbosity").
tipsy is a genteelism (see 85).

84   EATABLE, EDIBLE

   The adjectives **eatable** (Old English *etan*) and **edible**
(Latin *edibilis*) in their general meaning of "able to be
eaten" are synonymous and in some contexts could be interchanged, but they can have slightly different implications.
eatable usually implies the "damning with faint praise" of a
food that is able to be eaten though hardly with pleasure.
"The plums I bought today are somewhat over-ripe but they
are eatable." **edible**, which in this context would be pompous, generally refers to something that, though not commonly used as food, can be eaten without harm. "There are
many varieties of mushrooms, regarded by most people as
toadstools and as possibly poisonous, that are edible", and
there is e.g. "edible seaweed".

85   EDIFICE, BUILDING

   edifice, for **building**, in its concrete sense (generally with
reference to a large building), belongs to that class of words
to which *M.E.U.* has given the happy term "genteelisms".

A genteelism Fowler defines as the substitution, for the ordinary natural word that would first suggest itself to the mind, of a synonym thought to be less soiled by the common herd, less familiar, less plebeian, less vulgar, less improper. Genteelisms and formal words (see 15) are not always mutually exclusive.

In a figurative sense **edifice** can be an effective word. "Trotsky feared that the edifice of Russian Socialism might collapse under the pressure of the capitalist world long before it was completed."

EFFICIENT, EFFECTIVE, EFFICACIOUS, 86 EFFECTUAL

All four words express suitability for a purpose mentioned or implied. **efficient** and **effective** are used of either persons or things: an "efficient secretary", an "efficient tool"; an "effective speaker", an "effective scheme of decoration". **efficacious** and **effectual** are used only of things: an "efficacious drug", an "effectual barrier".

EGOIST, EGOTIST 87

Both words are often used to mean a selfish person, but when a distinction is preserved **egotist** generally refers to one who makes a practice of speaking about himself and his doings; **egoist** to one who looks upon all questions in their relation to himself. Sir Willoughby Patterne, in George Meredith's novel *The Egoist*, is not an **egotist**. Indeed the *Oxford English Dictionary* says that an **egoistic** man is not necessarily selfish. An **egotistic** man is.

END, FINISH, STOP, CONCLUSION, 88 TERMINATION, COMPLETION, CESSATION, CEASE

end, finish, and **stop** are the ordinary working words. **conclusion** and **termination** are on the formal side (see 15). **completion** implies that something is made whole or perfect.

"The commission had to question hundreds of witnesses before the completion of the inquiry." Compare the adjective **complete**: e.g. "a complete horseman".

Both **cease** and **cessation** ("coming to an end") are formal except in the phrases "without cease", "without cessation".

For verbs see 349.

Here, as elsewhere, this book cannot attempt to mention all the nice distinctions that in certain contexts may make one word more idiomatic than another though in many general applications they may be closely synonymous. Thus we would probably say with reference to a game that it "came to an end," of a train that it "came to a stop", and in neither case "came to a finish"; and "I must put a stop to this", or "an end to this", but not a "finish to this".

For verbs see 349.

89   ENDEAVOUR, TRY, STRIVE, ATTEMPT, SEEK

try is the ordinary working word. **endeavour** is on the formal side (see 15). It would be pompous to say "I shall **endeavour** to buy tickets for Saturday's performance". Nevertheless this three-syllabled word is often used where one might expect the shorter **attempt** or **try**. Perhaps, on an analogy with **difficult** (see 71), **endeavour** is unknowingly preferred (*a*) because **try** has many meanings, with 53 lines in *C.O.D.*, whereas **endeavour** has only three lines (compare also **alter**, 29; **expensive**, 101; **impecunious**, 149; **wealthy**, 311); and (*b*) because, for the idea of "trying hard", **endeavour** has in its length an onomatopoeic effect: compare again **difficult** and **consequence** (303).

strive means "make a great effort".
attempt is on the formal side.
seek=**try** today strikes an archaic note.

As a noun the relation of **try** to **endeavour** and **attempt** is different from its relation as a verb. **endeavour** and **attempt** are the ordinary working words, and **try** is used only colloquially or in a special sense in football. As with the verb, the noun **endeavour** is used more than **attempt**: perhaps again for its onomatopoeic effect; it is also more euphonious. Moreover it can be used in a general sense, whereas **attempt** is generally restricted to a particular action. "This account of the work of the navy is a story of high endeavour." On the other hand in certain phrases **attempt** as a noun is idiomatic, and **endeavour** could not be substituted: e.g. "at the first attempt", "a poor attempt".

For **try**=**test** see 373; for **seek**=**search for**, 321.

ENTRY, ENTRANCE 90

Both words are given in *C.O.D.* as meaning (*a*) the act of coming or going in; (*b*) the place at which one comes or goes in. Generally, however, today the word for (*a*) is **entry** ("The entry of the troops was postponed to October 1st"); and, for (*b*), **entrance** ("The entrance to the fair was by the western gate of the park").

We speak also of a large or small **entry** of competitors. **entrance** means also "right of admission", especially in an adjectival use; "entrance examination", "entrance fee".

EPIC, HEROIC 91

epic by etymology (Greek) means "narrative". As a noun it means an account, usually in verse, celebrating the achievements of one or more heroes of history or legend: e.g. the *Iliad* of Homer. Adjectively it means (1) suitable for narration in such a form, (2) **heroic** in type or scale. A person might conceivably be described as "an epic character;" the Battle of Britain could be called "an epic story", for that story would give an account of **heroic** passages in a historical event. As a vogue-word (see 34) **epic** is often debased. A famous golfer can make **heroic**, but not **epic**, efforts to beat his opponent; we may describe a lifeboat's attempt to rescue a drowning crew as heroic, but scarcely as epic; a book cannot properly be described as "an epic novel".

Compare **saga** (an old Norse word), which, by transference from its original meaning, is properly a story of heroic achievement, but is misused for merely **story, tale, account**: "So ran the prisoner's saga as she related to the court the course of events that had brought her into the dock".

92   EQUALITARIAN, EGALITARIAN

These words are not yet admitted to *C.O.D.*, but **equalitarian** is now fairly common, as an adjective corresponding to **equalitarianism**: the theory of the **equality** of human beings, or a belief in the desirability of institutions that promote equality. It is applied to persons or to policies.

egalitarian (a French word) with the same meaning is an affectation of journalese.

93   ERE, BEFORE

The use of **ere**, both as a conjunction and a preposition, for **before**, is an archaism.

94   ESQ., MR.

For legal or ceremonial purposes there still exist qualifications entitling a man to the designation of **esquire**. In practice, however, with the gradual weakening in the recognition of social distinctions, some of us today are often in doubt whether we ought to address an envelope to "A. Jones, Esq.", or "Mr. A. Jones". Others, influenced by strong beliefs in equality, regard "Esq." as a snob-word, and, unless the addressee is titled, use "Mr.", or avoid the issue by writing merely "A. Jones". The usage of government departments seems to vary. Outside the United Kingdom and Ireland: e.g. among Canadians and Australians, the word is hardly ever used.

Though these words could generally be interchanged without affecting the meaning, there are recognizable differences that in some contexts would make one of them the most suitable. **essential** is the strongest word of the three; **requisite** the weakest.

For a long analysis of the three words with examples see *M.E.U.*

EVACUATE, EMPTY, REMOVE   96

Before the last war to **evacuate** was restricted to the meaning of to **empty**, especially with reference to the stomach or the bowels. A town could be said to be **evacuated**, but not its inhabitants. Since the last war the use of the word has been extended to mean **remove** (transitive and intransitive) and **leave** (transitive). "The Council evacuated the children"; "The children were evacuated into the country"; "I evacuated to North Wales"; "Many mothers evacuated the big cities to join their children".

Time is needed to show which of these uses becomes established. The word does not seem to be used unless there is a general or forced movement in progress.

EXCEPTIONAL, UNUSUAL, ABNORMAL,   97
ANOMALOUS, MORBID

abnormal and **anomalous** are often used as pretentious substitutes for **exceptional** or **unusual**. **abnormal** is also sometimes used as a synonym of **morbid**, though that which is **exceptional, unusual**, may deviate from type in admirable ways: e.g. in physical strength; and genius is **abnormal** but not generally **morbid**.

EXCLUSIVE, SELECT   98

exclusive is a genteelism (see 85) with the underlying idea of "shutting out" persons or things regarded as undesirable. **select** rather suggests picking or choosing for excellence.

Until recently **executive** as a noun was used only for the branch of government that is concerned with "executing," carrying out, laws, regulations, etc., as contrasted, for example, with the legislature, the branch of the state that makes laws. An American use of the word is now becoming common here for an **officer** or **official** in a business organization, especially one who has a high post and important duties.

100   EXIGUOUS, SMALL

exiguous (Latin *exiguus*="scanty, barely sufficient") is a show-word (see 15) for **small**.

101   EXPENSIVE, DEAR, COSTLY

expensive and **dear** are the ordinary working words. There is a tendency to use the longer and Romance **expensive** in preference to the shorter and Saxon **dear**. This is probably because **expensive** has only one meaning, whereas **dear** has many. Compare **alter** (29), **difficult** (71), **endeavour** (89), **impecunious** (149), **wealthy** (311).

costly is generally used in a figurative sense. "Passchendale was probably the most costly battle in which the British army has ever been engaged." In a literal sense it is on the borderline of being a snob-word. Tennyson may have contributed to its discredit by the absurd effect of its use in the last lines of "Enoch Arden":

> And when they buried him the little port
> Had seldom seen a costlier funeral.

dear in a figurative sense is generally used adverbially. "This social lapse cost him dear, for he was never again invited to Holland House."

experiment can be used for (1) a single **experiment,** (2) a series of **experiments,** (3) the process of making **experiments. experimentation** is used in senses (2) and (3) by those who prefer six syllables to four.

EXPLOIT, WORK, USE, UTILIZE   103

work and **use** are the common working words. **exploit** today carries with it the idea of action that is thorough, i.e. of "working thoroughly," "using to the best advantage," "extracting the utmost benefit from" (e.g. a mine, a person). When that which is **exploited** is a person, the word generally has a bad sense: of turning that person to account for one's own ends, irrespective of, neglectful of, or in opposition to, his interests, in a selfish unscrupulous way. **utilize,** so far as it is not chosen instead of **use** by those who prefer a long word to a short one, means to put to a profitable purpose B when A is not available.

EXTREMELY, EXCEEDINGLY, EXCESSIVELY   104

extremely is derived from the Latin adjective *extremus*= "uttermost"; **exceedingly** and **excessively** from the Latin verb *excedere* (perfect tense *excess*—)="go beyond". **extremely** and **exceedingly,** however, are more closely synonymous with each other than either is with **excessively. extremely** and **exceedingly** are applied to adjectives or adverbs that have a good or bad or neutral implication. A person can be **extremely** or **exceedingly** generous, mean, busy; a thing can be done **extremely** or **exceedingly** well, badly, quickly. On the other hand **excessively** means going "too far": i.e. beyond what is desirable, and is therefore always used in a bad sense. Thus, whereas for a teacher to be said to be **extremely** or **exceedingly** strict would not necessarily imply an unfavourable criticism, for him to be said to be **excessively** strict would do so. So too a person might be said to enjoy being **extremely** or even **exceedingly** busy, but not **excessively** busy; and to be **extremely** or **exceedingly** kind, but not **excessively** kind (at all events unless it was implied in the context that by over-kindness somebody was being spoilt).

105   FACE, COUNTENANCE, VISAGE, PHYSIOGNOMY

face is the front of the head, thought of with reference to the various features that comprise it; **countenance** is the same part with reference to the expression it bears. "Her face was a perfect oval." "That morning my chief's countenance reflected his anxiety." **face** has many idiomatic uses.

visage is a formal word (see 15), chiefly literary, for **face** or **countenance**.

countenance is sometimes used with reference to a "composed look" in such phrases as "He kept his countenance"; "This remark put him out of countenance"; "I kept him in countenance by refusing to join in the laugh against him".

physiognomy is a facetious physiognomy.

106   FACE, FACE UP TO

face up to is verbosity. Thus in "It is time you faced up to the difficulty", the words **up to** do not add any meaning to the bare verb **face**. Compare **check up on** (40), **manned up** (196).

107   FACILE, EASY

facile is distinct from **easy** in having a depreciatory or contemptuous suggestion with reference to a person who does something, or to a thing that is done, with such ease that it brings little credit to the doer or is of little import: e.g. a **facile** versifier, a **facile** victory.

factor is used today as a maid-of-all-work for the meanings many other words have: e.g. **fact, circumstance, principle, consideration, cause, constituent, reason, element, influence, feature, point**. In many contexts the precise meaning is not clear.

FAMOUS, CELEBRATED, NOTED, NOTORIOUS,   109
NOTABLE, NOTEWORTHY, EMINENT

All these words have the general meaning of "well-known", but some of them have distinctive implications.

eminent refers only to persons; the other words to persons and things.

notable and **noteworthy** in some contexts mean "remarkable", "striking", or "worthy of being known".

eminent is used with reference only to what a person is or was while alive. The first Duke of Marlborough was **eminent** in his lifetime (and **famous**); today he is **famous** but not **eminent**.

notorious implies that what a person or thing is well known for are bad qualities (though the sense is not so strong as that underlying its antonym "infamous"). "Nero was notorious for his cruelty and tyranny."

FATAL, FATEFUL   110

fateful covers the idea of a destiny that is happy or unhappy. The first meeting with a woman one marries may be regarded as **fateful** whether the marriage turns out happily or unhappily. Sometimes, however, the word means nothing more than "important", "momentous": "A fateful evening doth descend on us" (Coleridge). **fatal** refers to that which is fraught with unhappy issues only. A "fatal step" has disastrous results, and cannot be retraced. When qualifying some words it implies that the unhappy issue is death: e.g. a "fatal (="mortal") wound or accident".

fault can refer to things, to persons, and to trained animals; **failing** and **foible** only to persons. A **fault** in a human being is morally censurable. **foible** (French: now obsolete for *faible*="weakness") is a weak point in a person's character, usually not of a grave sort, but regarded as a venial weakness, and so pardonable. Somewhere between the two comes a **failing**.

112   FEATURE, PORTRAY, DEPICT, DESCRIBE

portray and **depict** mean (*a*) "give a pictorial representation of"; (*b*), in its synonymous relation to **describe**, "give a verbal account of". **feature**, as a verb, goes back two centuries, and sixty years ago it was used with the meaning of "make a special feature; especially to exhibit as a prominent feature in a dramatic piece" (*Shorter Oxford English Dictionary*). It then easily came to be used with reference to films, for "show on the screen," in mentioning a particular actor's name. In recent years its use has been extended to the meaning of **describing** in print a prominent news item: "Criticisms have been made of the way in which the world's Press has featured the communal disorders in India"; and intransitively: "How is it that Gurevitsch remains among an obscure minority and Lysenko features in the headlines?"

113   FEMALE, FEMININE, WOMANLY, WOMANISH, EFFEMINATE

female (adjective) refers to the sex of a human being or other creature: a **female** servant, a **female** wolf.

feminine is restricted to human beings, and refers to qualities supposed to be typical of woman as contrasted with man.

womanly in some contexts is identical with **feminine**, but is usually restricted to admirable qualities: e.g. "womanly tenderness", "womanly sympathy". The Victorians used a phrase, "a womanly woman", to indicate one having such qualities to a high degree, and strong domesticity. On the other hand a misogynist would probably speak of "feminine weakness".

womanish and **effeminate** are always used in a bad sense with reference to the existence in a man of **feminine** qualities that in his sex are weak or despicable.

FEW, SOME, NUMBER, SEVERAL, DIVERS, 114 SUNDRY

some implies more than **few** or **a few**, and less than **a number** (of). A slight distinction in effect between **few** and **a few** (or **some few**) is that **few** implies an antithesis to **many**, whereas **a few** implies an antithesis to **none**. Thus "few prisoners escaped" emphasizes the fact that "not many", "hardly any", did so; but "a few escaped", that "not all" failed to do so.

The ideas of **few** and **many** are as strongly opposed to each other as those of any words can be, but there exist the absurd colloquialisms **quite a few** and **a good few**. These are used to mean, not a **few**, but on the contrary a **fair**, a **considerable**, a **good**, or even a **large**, number. Why not therefore say so instead of distorting the meaning of **few**?

sundry and **divers**, meaning **several**, are archaic. The Bible (*Hebrews* I, 1) in the Authorized Version has "God, who at sundry times and in divers places", which suggests that at one time the words had different meanings, but the translation in the Revised Version is "by divers portions and in divers manners." Shakespeare (*As You Like It*, III, ii, 328) has "Time travels in divers paces with divers persons," where there is the sense of "diverse in kind;" but as used today there is no distinction between the two words. The quaint phrase "all and sundry" (="one and all") survives.

115 FEWER, LESS

fewer is used of numerical quantity, **less** of quantity in bulk or size. "The fewer men, the greater share of honour." "There is less food and clothing nowadays than there was before the war." A common mistake is to use **less** when the word should be **fewer**: e.g. "No less than 80 members applied"; "There are less pupils per teacher in a class today than forty years ago".

116 FINALLY, ULTIMATELY

In some contexts the words could be interchanged. **finally**, however, can refer to a statement, e.g. in sermons: "And finally, brethren . . .", as well as to an action or **event**, whereas **ultimately** refers only to an action or event.

The adjectives **final** and, in its ordinary use, **ultimate** correspond in meaning to the adverbs. **ultimate**, however, has a special use in philosophical language, where, instead of meaning "last", it is used, e.g. in the phrase "ultimate cause", as a synonym of **primary**: i.e. **first, earliest**.

117 FLUCTUATE, VACILLATE

Both words mean to "vary irregularly". **vacillate** refers only to persons; **fluctuate** to persons or things. **vacillate** is generally used in a bad sense: e.g. with reference to an inability to reach a decision from weakness of character, or to changeableness in conduct due to absence of principle. An admirable person, however, may **fluctuate**: e.g. between hope and despair, not from weakness but because circumstances change.

118 FOLLOWING, AFTER

following, being a participle, needs a noun or pronoun with which to agree. "Following Nazi precedents the Soviet newspapers first gave warnings of what was about to be done by accusing their opponents of identical plans." The word is often used, however, as if it were a preposition, equivalent to **after**. Journalese and officialese are irked by such simple words as **after**. (Compare their preference for **prior to** to **before**.) "Following this information on the telephone, the man was arrested." This usage may become established, in the way that, with the meaning of **through, on account of**, the participle **owing** (to) has done. It might be urged in defence that sometimes, besides the meaning of sequence in time, which **after** primarily has, **following** can be useful for implying result. "Following many attempts the engine was at last got to start." "Following severe rains the fields were flooded." I am indebted to Sir Ernest Gowers, who in *Plain Words* deprecates the prepositional use of **following**, for a note on this matter. "I agree that those who use **following** for **after** often do so because they wish to imply *propter hoc* as well as *post hoc*, but I do not think this is a good excuse for inventing a new preposition. If a writer means *post hoc*, he should say **after**; if he means *propter hoc*, he should say **in consequence of** or **as a result of** or **in conformity with** or whatever phrase may precisely express his meaning."

FOOLISH, STUPID, SILLY   **119**

The common meaning of these words is "opposite to wise". In some contexts they would be closely synonymous, but, especially when applied to the general character of a person, rather than to a particular action, **stupid** often implies a person who is dull by nature, slow-witted, dense. On the other hand a person may be **foolish** or (somewhat colloquial) **silly** though by no means **stupid**. "Teresa Guiccioli was in some ways a silly woman, but not a stupid one."

forcible=(1) done by force: "They made a forcible entrance"; (2) effective, convincing, with general reference to a person or with special reference to manner, speech, literary style, etc.

forceful is described by *C.O.D.* as "archaic or literary or affected", for **forcible**.

121   FOREWORD, PREFACE, INTRODUCTION

foreword is a fairly recent invention, which, as a substitute for **preface**, with its long and honourable history, and the well-established word **introduction**, is generally a publisher's affectation. The term may be justifiable if **preface** and **introduction** have already been used for matter written by the author or by the editor proper, and additional preliminary matter is contributed by a distinguished person acting as sponsor of the book.

Perhaps the word came in to emphasize the shortness of a simple preparatory note in contrast with the lengthy **preface** that often appeared in Victorian books.

122   FORWARD, DISPATCH, TRANSMIT, SEND

dispatch with the meaning of **send**, and **forward** with that meaning unless it has a further implication (see below), are commercial jargon: e.g. "The goods will be dispatched (or forwarded) to-morrow". If, however, a person is e.g. absent from home, a letter sent to and arriving at his home can suitably be said to be **forwarded** to him. "The report, which was sent to London by special courier, has been forwarded to the Minister, who is now in Edinburgh." **transmit** is a show-word (see 15) for **send** unless it implies the action of A as an intermediary in **sending** to B something received from C.

As a noun, however, **dispatch** is convenient, for there is not a noun corresponding to the verb **send** unless the gerund, **sending**, is used.

friendship and **amity** always imply a mutual relation between persons. **friendliness** also can imply this: e.g. if followed by "between" ("There was great friendliness between us"); but it may refer only to feelings or action on one side: "He always showed great friendliness towards me". **amity** is a formal word (see 15).

FRIGHTEN, TERRIFY, ALARM, INTIMIDATE, 124 SCARE

To **frighten** is the general working word, which may imply the causing of various degrees of fear. To **terrify** is to **frighten** to an extreme degree. To **alarm** generally implies the causing of a milder degree of fear than to **frighten**: sometimes rather a state of extreme anxiety. To **intimidate** is a formal word (see 15) if used merely for to **frighten**, but it generally implies pressure, threat, bullying, with the object of influencing conduct. To **scare** implies the causing of sudden and often unreasoning fear, panic.

FUNCTION, ACT, WORK, OPERATE 125

function as a verb, if used at all, is best retained for biological and mechanical action. "The heart ceases to function at death"; "The engine now functioned perfectly"; "My refrigerator is not functioning satisfactorily". Otherwise, as a substitute for **act, work, operate** (e.g. "The Council was not empowered to function in this matter"), it is a show-word (see 15).

GARRET, ATTIC, LOFT 126

All three words mean the top storey of a building just below the roof, or a room in this. **garret** generally implies sordid circumstances. **loft** generally means an **attic** open to

the rafters, and a space not occupied by human beings, but
used for storing things: e.g. hay over a stable.

127 GIVE, PRESENT, DONATE, GIFT, BEQUEST

give is the ordinary working word. **present** in this sense
would be pompous for most purposes, but it can be suitable
with reference to a ceremonious occasion. You **give** your
friend a present; a millionaire **gives** twenty thousand pounds
to a charity; but the King **presents** a decoration, and "At the
last meeting at which he was to serve as Chairman the
Secretary presented him with a gold watch subscribed to by
members of the committee". **donate** Sir Alan Herbert calls
a "snob-word". To a beggar Mrs. Jones **gives** sixpence;
but in the local paper she may not be allowed to do anything less high-sounding than **donate** £5 to the Cottage
Hospital. Snobbery and gentility are linguistically first
cousins to each other, and second cousins to journalese.
gift, used as a verb, is one of the Americanisms that, as a
result of the presence of American forces in this country
during the war, have invaded our vocabulary. To **bequest**
is to give, leave, bequeath, by will.

With an inconsistency often found in language **present** as
a noun is the working word, whereas **gift** is on the formal
side (see 15) or commercialese; a shop will issue a "catalogue of Christmas Gifts". **donation** is an established word
for a sum of money given to a charity or other public cause.

Corresponding to the verbal use of **gift** there is a use of
loan as a verb. This *C.O.D.* gives as "chiefly U.S.," but the
larger Oxford Dictionaries mention it as going back to
Middle English, and it shows signs of becoming established
with distinctive reference to objects lent—to **loans** (noun)—
for exhibitions.

Both nouns mean a look that is brief. **glance** is the seeing, the looking at; **glimpse** is what is seen. So you "take" or "give" a **glance** at something, but "get" a **glimpse** of it. Indeed a **glimpse** is got by a **glance**.

GLOBAL, GLOBE, WORLD   129

global and (adjectivally) **globe** are now frequent, at all events in journalese and officialese, as synonyms of **world** in its adjectival use. On the other hand **global** is now often used in a sense, going back to the end of the nineteenth century, of **complete, entire, total**, without reference to conditions affecting the whole world. Thus with reference to negotiations between the Ministry of Health and the medical profession we read that a conference of doctors "calls upon the Minister of Health to state what global sum should in his opinion be in the central pool to implement the recommendations of the Spens Report". In neither sense do **global** and **globe** serve a useful purpose.

GOURMAND, GOURMET   130

Both words can be used to mean a connoisseur of cooking and delicate food, but **gourmand** is often used in a bad sense for a glutton.

GRATIS, GRATUITOUSLY, FREE   131

The adverbs **gratis** (Latin: contracted ablative plural of *gratia*="favour") and **gratuitously** (Latin: *gratuitus*= "spontaneous"), and the adjectives **gratis** (rarely so used) and **gratuitous**, are show-words (see 15) for **free, without charge, for nothing.**

Grecian is today almost obsolete except when applied to the architecture of the ancient Greeks and to the type of features immortalized by their sculpture, especially the nose. Everything else connected with ancient or modern Greece is **Greek**. *M.E.U.* mentions the **Grecian** bend in walking, the **Grecian** knot in dressing woman's hair, and **Grecian** slippers, but these hardly enter into talk or writing today. At Christ's Hospital the boys that reach the highest form are still called **Grecians**.

In the past **Grecian** was common. Troilus in *Troilus and Cressida* sighed his soul "towards the **Grecian** tents"; Sir Walter Scott wrote "And ne'er did Grecian chisel trace"; in Matthew Arnold's "Scholar-Gipsy" the Tyrian trader "saw the merry Grecian coaster come"; and there is Keats's "Ode on a Grecian Urn".

133 GUARANTEE, AGREE, ENSURE, ASSURE

To **guarantee** is strictly to give a "guaranty," a security for the fulfilment of conditions. A shop, selling you a watch, may **guarantee** its working satisfactorily by undertaking, if it fails to do this, to give you another or to take it back and return the purchase money. A person may **guarantee** the financial liability of a person by signing an agreement that in default he will be responsible for the amount. The word then came to be used in a more general way in the sense of **making certain, ensuring**, given conditions: "Only a strong British navy could guarantee the freedom of the seas"; or for formally **agreeing**, or merely **promising**, to carry out the terms of a contract, though no "guaranty" be given. The noun has come to be used in a similar way. "Dockers on strike have agreed to return to work provided that the employers guarantee no victimization." "The military government in the British zone pointed out that it had never given any guarantee that these industrial plants would remain in Germany." In a vulgar extension the verb is used, presumably with the underlying idea of staking one's reputation on the truth of what is said, as merely a synonym of **assure, state with conviction**: "I guarantee he will not keep that job long"; "My seed merchant guarantees I shall find that variety of pea satisfactory for late sowing"; "Guaranteed to be made from pure ingredients"; or, height of absurdity, "I guarantee it will be a fine day tomorrow for the outing". The noun is subjected to similar misuse, and sometimes with reference not to the future but to the past. "The blazing villages, huts, and anything that could give cover were by this evening a guarantee of ruthless but necessary destruction." Here **guarantee** means **proof, evidence**.

HABIT, CUSTOM 134

A **habit** is a way of behaving that has become fixed by repetition. A **habit** is usually personal. When **habits** common to many people are in question we speak of them as **customs**. (Compare the adjectives **habitual** and **customary**.) The celebration of Christmas is a **custom**. At a public dinner it is the **custom** not to smoke until the King's health has been drunk. Some people think that smoking is a bad **habit**.

HANGED, HUNG 135

The past tense and the past participle of **hang** in the sense of capital punishment by suspending on a gibbet are **hanged**. In all other senses the form is **hung**. Thus pictures and bacon are **hung**, murderers are **hanged**.

happen and **occur** are the working words that meet every ordinary need for the meaning of "come to pass," "take place".

Used with care **develop** has the idea of "unfolding," "coming from a latent to an active or visible state" (*C.O.D.*); **materialize** of "becoming actual fact". As synonyms of **happen** or **occur** without these implications the words should be avoided. **materialize** is often used in absurd extensions, as e.g. when we read in a newspaper that "the hoped-for thaw failed to materialize", and a few days later that "fortunately, when snowed-up streets would have been impassable to fire-engines, fires did not materialize".

eventuate is a long and clumsy show-word (see 15).

transpire in the sense of **happen**, **occur**, is journalese. By derivation it means, and, if it is used at all, it should be restricted to, the idea of "leak-out", "become known". "Cabinet secrets must not be allowed to **transpire**." "Although no official announcement had yet been made the news soon transpired that negotiations had broken down." The origin of the use of the word to mean **happen, occur**, is stated by the *Shorter Oxford English Dictionary* to have originated in America in 1804.

137 HAPPENING, EVENT, OCCURRENCE, INCIDENT, EPISODE, EVENTUALITY, CONTINGENCY, DEVELOPMENT

event and **occurrence** are the ordinary working words.

happening became popular about a quarter of a century ago. Fowler described it as an "unworthy literary or journalistic affectation . . . a child of art and not of nature." The second charge is without foundation, for though neither *C.O.D.* nor the *Shorter Oxford English Dictionary* gives it, the *Oxford English Dictionary* cites examples of its use in the plural (in which it is still mostly found) from the seventeenth to the nineteenth centuries.

People often seem to go out of their way to use it in preference to the shorter, simpler word **event**. Thus, whereas an official statement issued by a political body mentioned "recent events in Czechoslovakia", a writer in *The Times*, commenting on this report, and presumably scorning the dissyllable as too common and mean for his fine effects, preferred to speak of the "happenings" in that country. The popularity of the word is no doubt influenced partly by the partiality of journalese for long words, partly by the existence of the verb **happen**, whereas **event** has no corresponding verb if we except the atrocity **eventuate** (see last article).

No shadow of meaning distinct from that of **event** and **occurrence** is recognizable in ordinary speech or writing, but a friend in the country tells me that the inhabitants of the village where she lives commonly use **happening** with reference to everyday or trivial matters, and would reserve **event**, if used at all, to something important, as shown, for example, in the phrase "It is quite an event".

To sum up, it cannot be denied that **happening** is today used so widely, and sometimes by good writers, that it must be accepted as established, even if only, as some of us may think, as an elegant or inelegant variation.

No objection can be taken to the use of **happening** as a verbal noun: e.g. "Its happening just then took me by surprise"; let alone as a pure participle: "Happening to be in town that day I decided to call on him".

incident has often the implication of an **event** or **occurrence** that is not of high importance. "Under the excitement of the moment a war correspondent sometimes writes with too much emphasis of events that afterwards show themselves to have been but passing incidents."

episode often refers to a single and isolated event in a given series of **events**. A. J. Balfour, in a satirical conjecture of the judgment passed by superior beings on man's history, when human existence has disappeared from this earth, described them as thinking it "a rather discreditable episode in the life of one of the minor planets".

eventuality is journalese.

contingency is best kept for reference to a **possible event** in the future, but by the hankerer after long words it is often used for what has happened: e.g. "This unexpected contingency upset all our plans". Often in journalese it is **contingencies** that **develop** (see last article) in preference to **events** that **happen**.

development should be restricted to the same sense as the verb **develop**.

138   HECTIC, EXCITING, WILD

hectic as an adjective (it is also a noun) is strictly an epithet applied to a fever of which a symptom is flushed cheeks; thence "morbidly flushed" (literally and metaphorically). Today it is widely used with the meanings of **exciting, wild**. "We spent a hectic evening at the party last night." "There was a hectic rush to pack and catch the train." *C.O.D.* enters this use as slang. It is, however, found in these senses among good writers: e.g. "Even Death moves swiftly in hectic highstepping New York" (E. V. Lucas).

The question arises why it is thought that some words and not others should be kept to their "strict" meaning. Why, for instance, should **hectic** not be used in these senses? No satisfactory reason can be given. Other words in the development of the language have had their literal meanings stretched. On what grounds can further stretchings be opposed? The middle-aged and the old among us have special need to be on their guard against refusal to accept changes. It is natural for them to feel that the vocabulary with which they have got on adequately for a long span of years is good enough for the rest of their own lives, and for the rising generation. For an attempt to formulate some principles in this matter see 196.

HELP, AID, ASSIST, SUCCOUR   **139**

help is the general working word. **aid** is on the formal side (see 15). **assist** also, if used as a mere substitute for **help** without any distinctive implications, is formal, but (by derivation "take one's stand by") it can have a useful shade of meaning by suggesting a subordinate rôle in the person giving help, or the giving of help in a habitual capacity, or both. A magistrate always has a clerk of the court to **assist** him; and we should describe him as an **assistant** rather than a **helper**. **succour** (by derivation "run to the help of") has a special use in a military sense, of bringing **help** to a place that is besieged; otherwise, somewhat rhetorical, it implies that the help given includes sympathy and comfort.

HITHER, HERE   **140**

hither for **here** is an archaism. (**thither**, *M.E.U.* points out, can be useful where ambiguity would result from **there**: e.g., in a guide book, "The road thither leaves the main road at right angles").

HOPELESS, DESPERATE   **141**

hopeless=without any hope; **desperate**=with extremely little hope. A venture that is **desperate** may come off; one that is **hopeless** cannot, for, if it were to do so, it could not have been **hopeless**, though it might have been thought to be so. **hopelessly** and **desperately** are related to each other in a similar way. "**hopelessly** ill"= so ill that there is no hope of recovery; "**desperately** ill"=so ill that hope of recovery and fear of death are equal. For **hopeless** see also 248.

142 HORRIBLE, AWFUL, TERRIBLE, DREADFUL, FEARFUL, FRIGHTFUL, HORRID, TERRIFIC, TREMENDOUS

All these words are used today much more commonly in the trivial sense of "disagreeable" than with their original meaning of inspiring horror, awe, etc. Now and then they may still be used by careful writers in their primary grave and dignified sense. "At that period a convert to Roman Catholicism like John Henry Newman was looked on by many English Protestants with awful curiosity", i.e. with "curiosity mingled with awe" (*The Times Literary Supplement*, 1948); "This argument and the awful weight of the hour quelled the would-be heresy hunters" (Mr. Winston Churchill in *Their Finest Hour*). Without exaggeration or perversion of their primary senses a "difficulty" might properly be said to be "tremendous"; a "prospect" (figuratively), "dreadful"; a "crime", "horrible", and so on. More often, however, the sort of thing we hear or even read is that "The food at the hotel was horrible"; "We had awful weather"; "She is a horrid creature"; "It was a terrible (or dreadful or fearful or frightful) pity he missed that catch"; "He had tremendous knowledge of the subject".

A few familiar instances from literature of the effective use of these words in their original sense are sufficient to show what a loss to the language is threatened if they continue to be abased in their present trivial uses.

O horrible, O horrible, most horrible! (Shakespeare: *Hamlet*)

> Death, be not proud, though some have called thee
> Mighty and dreadful. (Donne)

> What immortal hand or eye
> Could frame thy fearful symmetry? (Blake)

> Because he knows a frightful fiend
> Doth close behind him tread. (Coleridge)

> Beneath whose awful hand we hold
> Dominion over palm and pine. (Kipling)

The adverbs are generally used merely as emphasizers corresponding somewhat to the use of "bloody" among those for whom a day is "bloody hot" or "bloody cold". Absurdity is reached when the primary use of the adverb is contradictory to that of the adjective: e.g. "awfully jolly", "frightfully pretty", "dreadfully kind". Perhaps the most commonly used of these words in both a good and a bad sense, and both adjectivally and adverbially, are **tremendous** and **tremendously**: a "tremendous pity", a "tremendous advantage", "tremendously pleased", "tremendously disturbed".

HUMAN, HUMAN BEING 143

The *Shorter Oxford English Dictionary*, citing the substantival use of **human** (=**human being**) as far back as 1553, adds "now chiefly jocular or affected". In recent years, however, this usage (especially in the plural) has become common in ordinary speech and writing. When we find even Mr. Ivor Brown using it, it would seem that the convenience of one word and two syllables over four words and four syllables has won the day, and that the noun must be regarded as established.

There is an analogy with **animal**, which is used both as adjective and noun.

HYPOCRITE, DISSEMBLER, DISSIMULATOR 144

In a general sense a **hypocrite** pretends to be what he is not; a **dissembler** or a **dissimulator** pretends not to be what he is. **hypocrite** has the further implication that a person makes a parade of the virtue he does not possess. Pecksniff in Dickens's *Martin Chuzzlewit* is an arch-**hypocrite**. In making a parade of virtue he does not possess he turns to advantage the vices he implicitly affects to condemn.

dissembler is more common than the longer word **dissimulator**. On the other hand the verb **dissimulate** is more common than **dissemble**: perhaps, as *M.E.U.* suggests, on account of the existence of the noun **dissimulation** and of the contrasting verb **simulate**.

145   IF, THOUGH, ALTHOUGH, BUT

if is often used elliptically when there is no explicit logical connection between the protasis (the **if**, conditioning, clause) and the apodosis (the result). "The hotel is certainly comfortable if rather dear." There is no true condition here justifying the use of **if** unless one understands the sentence to mean something such as "I can say that the hotel is certainly comfortable even if I have to add that it is dear", or "If I have to complain that the hotel is dear, I must in fairness admit that it is comfortable". Why not simply "although", or "though"? "The work was interesting if hard". Why not "although", or "though", or "but"? Absurdity is reached when one reads "If Dickens is often sickly sentimental, Thackeray is sometimes repellantly cynical".

146   ILLEGIBLE, UNREADABLE, INDECIPHERABLE, UNDECIPHERABLE

illegible refers to handwriting that is so ill-formed as to be impossible or extremely hard to make out. **unreadable** can also mean this, but it refers also to a composition so ill-expressed, dull, etc., that one is not interested enough to read it. **indecipherable** and **undecipherable**, when applied to handwriting, mean impossible to be made out, but both can refer also to hieroglyphics, and figuratively to other than written things of which the meaning is obscure or perplexing. For handwriting **illegible** is the word commonly used.

illness and **sickness** refer in a general way to bad health. **disease** refers to a particular kind of **illness** or **sickness**, with special symptoms and name. **malady** and **ailment**, closely synonymous with **disease**, are now rarely used. Journalese and genteelism prefer to describe Mr. Jones as being prevented from attending a meeting, not "by illness" or "because he is unwell", but "by indisposition", or "because he is indisposed".

immediately, instantly and **directly** are closely synonymous. "When he heard of my financial straits, he immediately came to my help (or instantly came to my help, or came to my help directly)." But **directly** is used less than **immediately** and **instantly**, perhaps because it has another meaning of "in a direct way".

instantaneously is used where the implication is that one thing happens in such a minute point of time after another that they seem almost simultaneous. "Everyone within a hundred yards of the explosion was instantaneously killed."

forthwith today has an archaic air but survives in officialese.

Besides these adverbial uses **immediately** and **directly** are used colloquially as conjunctions equivalent to "as soon as". "Immediately she came into the room the dog flew at her." "Directly she saw him she turned away."

straightway is archaic; **straightaway** is slang.

right away and **right off** are chiefly U.S.A.

Both **impecunious** and **indigent** are on the formal side
(see 15) for **poor**, but perhaps are sometimes chosen through
having only one meaning whereas **poor** has several. Com-
pare **alter** (29), **difficult** (71), **endeavour** (89), **expensive** (101),
wealthy (311).

penurious is generally used now with the sense, not of
poor, but of **stingy**, though the noun **penury** is a (somewhat
formal) synonym of **poverty**.

150   IMPERTINENT, INSOLENT, IMPUDENT, SAUCY, CHEEKY

insolent implies a higher degree of rudeness and offensive-
ness than **impertinent** or **impudent**. **impudent** refers to rudeness from an inferior to a superior. **saucy** and **cheeky** are
colloquial for **impudent**.

151   IMPLEMENT, COMPLETE, FULFIL

implement, from its formal meaning of **complete** (a contract), **fulfil** (an engagement), etc., has become a vogue-
word (see 34), with the meanings "make effective", "carry
out", "translate into action", a policy, act of parliament,
scheme, intention, promise.

implement is a useful word in its original meaning of
completing a contract, **fulfilling** a formal engagement, etc.,
but in recent years it has come into such widely-spread use,
with reference, not only to acts of parliament, resolutions of
committees, statements of policy, etc., but to schemes, aims,
intentions, proposals, or even private promises or trivial
arrangements, that those of us who wish to avoid vogue-
words (see 34) may well prefer to fall back on some such
phrases as "carry out", "make effective", "translate into
action".

To **imply** is to **mean**, but to convey the meaning implicitly rather than explicitly. To **insinuate** has the sense of conveying meaning in an indirect way: of hinting, suggesting obliquely, innuendo. **connote** is often used loosely for **mean**. In its precise sense it is used, with reference to a particular word, for **implying** something in addition to what primarily it **means**. Thus, with reference to something done so easily that its accomplishment reflects little credit, the word "facile" **means** "easy", and **connotes** contempt. *C.O.D.* gives **infer** as, in a secondary sense, equivalent to **imply**, and the *Oxford English Dictionary* quotes Milton and John Stuart Mill—two hundred years apart—as so using it, but today it is generally confined by careful speakers and writers to the sense of drawing a logical conclusion from facts or premises=**deduce** (see 58).

IMPOSSIBLE, INTOLERABLE, UNWORKABLE, 153
INCREDIBLE

Strictly, **impossible** and **intolerable** have widely different meanings: **impossible**, "unable to be", "unable to happen;" **intolerable**, "unable to be borne" (absolutely, or with the idea of "with patience"), or, loosely used, "disgraceful", "outrageous".

impossible, in a colloquial ellipsis, which is creeping into newspapers and books, is used as a synonym of **intolerable** with reference to a person with whom it is **impossible** to have satisfactory relations, or a situation that it is **impossible** to endure. In other extensions it is applied to a plan, idea, etc., that it is **impossible** to entertain seriously, or that is **unworkable**; or to a story, explanation, **impossible** to be believed, **incredible**.

154 IMPOSTOR, CHARLATAN, QUACK

All three words apply to a person who pretends to have what he has not or to be what he is not. **impostor** is a general word, and includes the senses of **charlatan** and **quack**. The pretensions of a **charlatan** are restricted to those in the realm of ideas: to pretending to have knowledge they have not. If this pretended knowledge is in medical matters a person is often given the specific name of **quack**, and in an adjectival use of that word he is said to prescribe **quack** remedies.

155 IMPRISON, INCARCERATE, INTERN

The common idea of **incarcerate, intern**, and, when it is used synonymously, **imprison**, is to keep people under guard so that escape is impossible. **imprison** is the general working word, though **put in prison** or **send to prison** is more common with reference to a criminal in a jail. **incarcerate** is a formal word (see 15) for **imprison** in jail. **intern**, used especially with reference to aliens in war time, means to keep in a detention camp.

imprison is used also with reference to inability to escape from a situation other than one enforced by man: e.g. to coal miners in a pit accident, and to animals in a cage; and figuratively: e.g. of a person whose mind may be described as being **imprisoned** by narrow prejudices.

156 IN, AT

With reference to the names of places, **in** is used for capitals and other cities; **at** generally for towns and villages. A person would be said to live **in** Edinburgh, Rome, Manchester; **at** Brighton, Henley, Shere (a village). When, however, people refer to their own presence or residence, they sometimes use **in** for a small place, perhaps because, as Pearsall Smith suggests, it then bulks more largely in their imagination. On the other hand there is also

an exception to the general principle of the use of **in** for
cities, for in mentioning famous buildings we speak, e.g.,
of the Pantheon **at** Rome, the Acropolis **at** Athens, the
Pump Room **at** Bath: **at** here being almost equivalent to **of**.

INABILITY, DISABILITY   157

Both words mean a lack that prevents a person from
doing something, but **disability** is restricted (*a*) to lack caused
by injury (compare "disabled"; and there are "disability
pensions" for military service after a war), or inherent
defect; (*b*) to legal disqualification.

INCIDENTALLY, PASSINGLY   158

Occasionally we find **incidentally** put to a useful use as a
synonym of **passingly**. "The Headmaster in taking the boy
to task for his low place in form incidentally referred to his
unpunctuality in arriving at school." In the most common
use of the word, however, there is an elision of some such
statement as "I may add that", "It is to be noted that", "I
omitted to mention that". "She took her departure.
Incidentally, I was never to see her again." "His rank at
that time, incidentally, was only that of captain." "The
inspector in charge of the inquiry into the disaster had himself been, incidentally, at one time an engine driver." "It
was from Mr. Smith that the bitterest criticism came.
Incidentally, Mr. Smith will next year be President of the
Association."
In these examples commas have been placed by the writer
to separate the adverb from the words they do not qualify,
but often this fails to be done, with momentarily absurd
effect until one realizes that it is not the event concerned
that is **incidental** but the writer's mention of it. "The
inspector in charge of the inquiry into the disaster had himself been incidentally at one time an engine driver." If a

matter is relevant, it can be stated without excuse; if it is not, it should be omitted.

As Fowler puts it in his pithy and sarcastic style, "**Incidentally** is now very common as a writer's apology for an irrelevance. Naturally those who find it most useful are not the best writers".

159   INCREDIBLE, UNBELIEVABLE

incredible (Latin *incredibilis*="unable to be believed"), when used in its strict sense, and **unbelievable**, are as closely synonymous as words can be. **incredible**, however, is often used with reference, not to something that cannot be, and therefore is not, believed, but to something that is so surprising, strange, abnormal, etc., that, though it is grudgingly accepted as true, it is hard to believe. "He accused the Ministry of incredible mismanagement." If it is impossible to believe that the mismanagement occurred, what grounds are there for an accusation? An article in a newspaper condemning a crime, which the writer thereby shows he does believe has been committed, is headed "Incredible Crime". This usage would force us to fall back on the longer and clumsy word **unbelievable** for what is not able to be believed.

The adverb **incredibly** also has extensions in which it is used to mean, not strictly **unbelievably**, but **almost unbelievably**, or to serve merely as an emphasizer, equivalent to **extremely**, etc. "That was an **incredibly** mean thing to do."

160   INDIVIDUAL, PERSON

An **individual** is a **person** mentioned in explicit or implicit contrast with a body of people: the family, the state, society generally. "The injustice done to an individual is sometimes of service to the State" (Junius). "The rule is on the whole a salutary one, even though here and there a few individuals may suffer hardship from it." "Individuals will be entitled to exchange the old currency up to 70 marks": i.e. businesses, etc., will come under other regulations. The word should be restricted to this use. Early in the nineteenth century, however, under the impulse of what the Fowlers in *The King's English* call "polysyllabic humour", **individual** was seized upon as a facetious substitute for **person** (in the plural, **persons** or **people**). Then it spread to speakers and writers using it without facetious intention, and the misuse became common. "He is a strange individual." "Several individuals came into the room whom I did not know." "In choosing the career of writing an individual must be prepared to risk for many years a precarious livelihood."

INQUIRE, ASK, DEMAND   161

In many contexts **inquire** would be on the formal side (see 15): e.g. "inquire the way," "inquire the price." There is, however, a natural tendency to use it in preference to **ask**, because it has a corresponding noun, **inquiry**, whereas **ask** has not; and because **ask** is often used in another sense= **request**, for giving expression to a wish, sometimes equivalent to an order: "He asked me to telephone to tell him the result of the interview"; "I asked the foreman to arrange to finish the work so as to be out of the house by the end of the week". **demand** is to **ask** for as a right, peremptorily or urgently. (For **demand** in another sense see 215.)

INSURE, ENSURE, ASSURE   162

ensure and **assure** in their synonymous use mean "make certain the happening of." **ensure** is more common, probably because **assure** can mean also "tell confidently of a thing, of its being so, that it is so." (**assure** has in this sense a corresponding noun, **assurance**; **ensure** has not.)

In a commercial sense the verbs **insure**, **assure**, and the nouns **insurance**, **assurance**, refer to a compact by which a specified sum is payable in certain contingencies, especially loss of or damage to property by fire, accident, unemployment, illness, death. So far as there is any distinction, **assurance** is restricted to the contingency of death; **insurance** refers to other risks. It has been pointed out by a writer on the history of the subject that, if the term **fire insurance** is to be used, then **life insurance** (instead of **life assurance**) is a misnomer, because it is not against **life** that one **insures**, but against **death**. Nevertheless, though a few firms entitle themselves **life assurance companies**, the usual term is **life insurance**, perhaps partly because **insurance** has only one meaning (always with reference to the payment of compensation), whereas **assurance** (see above) has also a use without this meaning.

163   INTENSE, INTENSIVE

intense=having some quality or feeling in a high degree: e.g. "intense admiration", "intense cold".

intensive=concentrated: e.g. "intensive study", "intensive cultivation" of ground. What is **intense** can be, but is not necessarily, **intensive**; what is **intensive** will generally be also **intense**. Thus in war in a bombardment the fire might be **intense**, but distributed over a wide objective, and therefore not **intensive**; or on the other hand it might be **intense**, and concentrated on a narrow objective, and therefore also **intensive**. If we were told only that the fire was **intensive**, we would generally correctly infer that it was **intense**.

164   INTERMEDIARY, MEDIATOR

The common idea of these words is that of a person acting as an agent, connecting link, go-between, for two parties. **intermediary** is the more general word. **mediator** is restricted to a person who intervenes for the purpose of reconciling two parties at variance.

interrogate is a formal word (see 19), and should be restricted to a close and thorough process of questioning by the police, in a law court, etc.

INTRIGUE, INTEREST, PUZZLE 166

To **intrigue** is primarily to carry on an underhand plot, employ secret influence (with), have a liaison (with). It is now a vogue-word (see 34)—a "modern Gallicism" the *Oxford English Dictionary* calls it—used with the meaning of **interest** and sometimes **puzzle**: sometimes as a participial adjective, **intriguing**. Even if it may sometimes convey an idea of exciting keen amusement, puzzled attention, curiosity, that **interest, puzzle,** etc., do not, it is tiresomely overworked.

INVOLVE, ENTAIL 167

involve and to a less extent **entail** are vogue-words (see 34) used loosely as synonyms of a number of words and phrases: **mean, cause, necessitate, need, lead to,** etc. Sir Ernest Gower in *Plain Words* describes **involve** as tired out by being put to every sort of base purpose, and needing a complete rest for a time in the hope that it may recover from its present invertebrate state and recapture something of its old vigour.

IRONY, SARCASM, SATIRE 168

irony is the use of words expressing the opposite of what is meant by a speaker or writer who knows that his real meaning will be understood. So the statement is made more emphatic. Thus in his funeral speech over Caesar's dead body Antony constantly refers to the conspirators as "honourable men".

sarcasm (literally="flesh-tearing") is the use of a wounding remark, a bitter sneer or jibe used in scorn or contempt:

indeed the essence of **sarcasm** is the intention of giving pain by bitter words. The speaker or writer means precisely what he says, but expresses himself with a bitterness that is intended to be offensive. Thus Locke writes: "If ideas were innate, it would save much trouble to many worthy persons". Speaking of the Pharisees and their ostentatious giving of alms, Christ said that in the glory of men "they have received their reward": an example of a **sarcasm** that is gentle.

satire is the use of ridicule in order to castigate vice or folly. The great Roman poet Juvenal **satirizes** human ambition, and Dr. Johnson adapts the **satire** in *The Vanity of Human Wishes*.

169 IRRITATING, ANNOYING, EXASPERATING, AGGRAVATING

In their primary use **exasperate** (Latin *exasperare*="to make rough") and **aggravate** (Latin *aggravare*="to make heavy") mean "intensify", "make worse". In this sense **exasperate** is almost obsolete; **aggravate** is still used: "These conditions will aggravate the disease"; "His lying aggravates the offence". **exasperating**, however, and **aggravating** have for long been used as synonyms of **irritating** and **annoying**. In this sense **exasperating** seems to have become established. **aggravating** has generally been restricted to colloquial use and has been regarded in writing as a vulgarism. Dickens helped to popularize it. Sir Ernest Gowers in *Plain Words*, citing for this use the "unimpeachable authority" of Dr. G. M. Trevelyan in a passage quoted, says that the word may now claim victory to be in sight for general acceptance in this sense. But victory will only provide a variation from three established words that have the same meaning, and this superfluous addition to the vocabulary will tend to the loss of the word in its distinctive and useful sense. Compare **anticipate** (7), **protagonist** (272).

In military language **issue** (=**supply**) is used in the passive, followed by "with". For "The necessary equipment was issued to the recruits", or "The recruits were issued the necessary equipment", the phrasing is "The recruits were issued with the necessary equipment". This usage with its superfluous preposition has crept into general use, especially since the war: e.g. we are told in a Government announcement that "the public is to be issued with a new identity card"; and in a further extension the verb is used transitively followed by **with**: "The Communists have issued foreign residents with permits to travel to Tientsin".

JOCOSE, JOCULAR, FACETIOUS, COMIC, 171 COMICAL, FUNNY

jocose, jocular, facetious refer to mirth roused only by what is said or written, whereas **comic, comical, funny** can refer also to the mirth roused by acts, appearance, character, etc. **facetious** implies levity that is ill-timed or otherwise inappropriate.

JUDICIAL, JUDICIOUS 172

judicial refers to judges, the administration of the law, and legal judgments. **judicious** in its most common use refers to the quality of being wise and prudent, of having good judgment. So far the words are not synonymous. **judicious**, however, *M.E.U.* points out, comes near in meaning to **judicial**, when it is applied to conduct, opinion, etc., that is well-weighed, wise, impartial, and so such as might be expected of a judge.

JUDGE, ADJUDICATE 173

In contexts where **judge** is not used with the meaning of "form an opinion," the words could often be interchanged.

With reference, however, to an issue in a court of justice **judge** is more common, whereas in a non-legal sense **adjudicate** is generally used: e.g. with reference to contests between competitors in athletic sports or at musical or dramatic festivals.

174   KILL, SLAY, MURDER, MASSACRE, SLAUGHTER, ASSASSINATE, DECIMATE

To **kill** is to deprive of life, to put to death, in any way. To **slay**, now somewhat archaic, generally implies killing in combat. To **murder** is to kill, with premeditation, in violation of the law. To **massacre** is general, mass killing. To **slaughter** is closely synonymous in many contexts with to **massacre**, but it is used also especially for the killing of animals for food (compare the noun **slaughter-house**). To **assassinate** is used of killing for political motives thought by the killer to justify the act. To **decimate** originally and etymologically (Latin *decem*=ten) meant to kill one in ten, and was used of a general employing this procedure to punish murderous or cowardly soldiers. Then for "one-tenth" there came to be substituted the general idea of "a large number", and used today it means to cause death to a large part of a given body of people. Moreover it is not restricted to the action of human agents, as are **slay**, **murder, massacre, slaughter, assassinate**. Plague or famine can be said to **decimate**. A loose extension of this general meaning of the word is used colloquially, and sometimes appears in journalese and inferior novels, with the sense of **shatter, shock, overwhelm, devastate**, especially in the present participle as an adjective. "What a decimating thought!" "She was plunged into despair by this decimating news."

knowledgeable in its primary passive meaning for what is capable of being known goes back to the early seventeenth century. The endings -able, -ible, are much more often applied to words (generally verbs, but here a noun) to form adjectives with a passive than an active meaning: e.g. "obtainable"="to be obtained," "manageable"="to be managed", "wearable"="to be worn". For **knowledgeable** in an active sense of, not a thing that is known, but a person who knows, the *Oxford English Dictionary* cites an example in 1831, as a colloquialism. The use has now crept into the written language, as a synonym of **well-informed**, or, sometimes, **intelligent**, or even **clever** or **learned**. Perhaps it became popular because it provided a substitute for "knowing", which carries a bad sense (as e.g. in "He is a knowing sort of person"). It is, however, a long and clumsy word; it does not fill a need in the language, for there exist well-established words or phrases serving for the meanings in which it is used; and the precise sense is not always clear. In its latest extension it is applied not only to people but to things: a book, lecture, etc. "This reprint includes a most knowledgeable essay by the editor".

LATE, BELATED   176

belated is restricted to the idea of delay that is undesirable or culpable. **late** does not necessarily imply this. "I prefer a late holiday in the autumn."

LATEST, LAST, LATTER, LATE   177

Both **latest** and **last** are superlatives of **late**, but **latest** has the implicit qualification of "up to now", whereas **last** is absolute, i.e. "final". The "latest news" does not means there will not be more news: "the last days of Hitler" refer to the end of his existence.

latter refers to the second mentioned of only two persons or things. "My sister and her husband joined me in the car, but in order to keep a business appointment the latter had to leave us at Birmingham." It is often incorrectly used with reference to more than two: "Of my three brothers, Albert, William and John, the latter emigrated to Australia"; "Some were listening to the radio; some reading; others playing darts: we joined the latter".

latter has two other misuses. (1) It is used instead of **late**, **latest**, **last**. "In the latter half of August there was little sun to ripen outdoor tomatoes." "This came into vogue in the latter days of the nineteenth century." "The latter years of the Roman Republic." (**latter** has, however, an established use in the compound **latter-day**, meaning **modern**.) (2) It is used with reference to only one antecedent: i.e. instead of "he," "him," "this," etc. "On Tuesday I visited my uncle; I found the latter looking much better."

For **last** see also 116.

178   LAZY, IDLE, INDOLENT, SLOTHFUL

The sense in which the four words (**slothful** is today not often used) are synonymous is that of being "unwilling to work", "avoiding work", "averse from effort". **indolent** and **slothful**, however, always have a bad implication, which **idle** and **lazy** need not have. A person can be **idle** from no fault of his. Thus if he is unemployed through depression in his trade he is not "unwilling to work" but "without work", "unable to work". **lazy**, too, has a use with no bad implications in such a context as "This year I am determined to spend a thoroughly lazy holiday" (i.e. in a justifiably inactive way).

idle means also "useless", "ineffective", "vain", "worthless", as e.g. in Tennyson's song in "The Princess": "Tears, idle tears"; and William Morris's "idle singer of an empty day".

idle has the verb "to **idle**"; **lazy**, for verb, has the colloquialism "to **laze**".

long is the general working word. **lengthy** is generally restricted to spoken and written matter, and implies that the speaker or writer is long to an excessive and tedious extent: compare **long-winded.**

LETTER, NOTE, COMMUNICATION,   180
FAVOUR, EPISTLE, MISSIVE, SCREED

note, in its synonymous relation to **letter,** means a short, and often informal, one. For correct uses of **communication** see dictionary. For a **letter** received it is official and commercial jargon. **favour** is another word in commercial jargon for a **letter** received containing an order or inquiry. **epistle** and **missive** (a favourite word in Victorian novels and plays) are archaic. **screed** is today a facetious term for a **letter** that is long.

LIBEL, SLANDER, CALUMNY, DEFAMATION   181

In English law **libel** and **slander** are distinct forms of defamation (see 1). The main difference is that **libel** is written and **slander** is spoken. In ordinary non-legal speech and writing this distinction is not preserved, and **libel** and **slander** are used indiscriminately except that **libel** is the word that tends to be applied with reference to accusations of the graver sort. **calumny** as a synonym of **libel** and **slander** is now seldom used.

LIFELONG, LIVELONG   182

lifelong means "lasting all one's life;" "He had a lifelong interest in ballet"; "Mary was her lifelong friend". **livelong** is only an intensive form of "long". It is rarely used now except in poetry and the phrase "the livelong day" (the whole length of the day).

The *Oxford English Dictionary*, which gives examples from Shakespeare, Southey, Newman, and Morris of the conjunctival use of **like**=**as**, and admits that the use is to be found in recent writers of standing, condemns it as now vulgar and slovenly. *M.E.U.* says that the speaker and writer deciding to use it "will be able to defend himself for using it; but also, until he has done so, will be condemned". Probably there is a natural tendency to prefer **like** on account of the many meanings in which **as** is used, e.g.= **because**; =**when**; =**which**; correlatively (**as** . . . **as**); parenthetically ("**as** I said"). Moreover **like** has a more substantial sound than the shorter and lighter word. Perhaps also familiarity with the American use of **like**=**as**, in the cinema and in popular songs, e.g. "Loving you like I do", will prevent many from learning or continuing to use **as**.

184   (a) LIKELY (adjective), PROBABLE;   (b) LIKELY (adverb), PROBABLY

(a) The adjectives **likely** and **probable** are closely synonymous in meaning, but idiomatically there is a tendency to restrict **likely** to negative, superlative, and predicative uses. Thus "That is a likely thing for him to have said", "A likely result will be his resignation", would be less idiomatic than if **probable** were used; but **likely** would be equally idiomatic in "That is not a likely thing for him to have said", "A very likely result will be his resignation", "Do you think that likely?"

likely, in distinction from **probable**, has a construction followed by the infinitive. "He is not likely to arrive today."

(b) A distinction between the adverbs **likely** and **probably** is that **likely** is not idiomatic, as **probably** is, unless qualified by another adverb: e.g. **very**, **quite**, **not**. A train, which can "probably be late", can also "most likely" be late: it cannot idiomatically "likely be late". Scottish idiom is looser in this usage.

limited, past participle of the verb **limit,** means "confined within bounds". As most things in the world are in this sense **limited,** it is a word that with strict meaning, used absolutely, could hardly ever add any meaning to a noun. It is commonly used loosely as equivalent to **small,** in the sense of too small for what is or might be desirable or needed. "My acquaintance with him is limited." "My time there was limited." A firm will advise prospective buyers to give their orders for an article at once "as supplies are limited" (often the phrase is "strictly limited"). Precise speakers and writers will be on their guard in the use of this word.

In the two current established uses of **liquidate** the word means (1) pay, clear off, a debt; (2) adjust the affairs of a firm or company on its dissolution, wind it up: i.e. bring it to an end. With an extension of this second meaning the verb **liquidate** and the noun **liquidation** have become vogue-words (see 34) in the sense of **remove, abolish, suppress,** etc. "An agreement on the liquidation of Prussia was the first and probably the easiest success of the four foreign Ministers in Moscow." "The Deputy Military Governor of the British Zone in Germany said that twenty-nine war plants were already liquidated." Mr. Ivor Brown in *No Idle Words* quotes a politician as describing the teaching of children as the "liquidation of illiteracy". This vogue-use covers also the meaning of **removing** a person or body of persons, especially political opponents, by killing. **liquidate,** says Sir Ernest Gowers in *Plain Words,* is now being used for the "ending of everything, from giving an employee notice to massacring".

eliminate in its primary sense means **remove.** In a tennis tournament **elimination** takes place after each round: i.e. the less successful do not compete again. The verb and noun are

now often used in much the same way as **liquidate** and
liquidation in their vogue-senses, as pretentious substitutes
for **remove, abolish, prevent, stop,** etc., and their nouns.
"This practice has been eliminated by the charge of a
deposit." "An international organization is needed by
which governments could co-operate in the elimination of
disease in animals used for food."

Often the word is ambiguous, when in a given context it
is not clear in which of its senses, of removing by killing or
without killing, it is used.

187   LIST, INCLUDE, MENTION

list as a verb, meaning "make a list", "compile a catalogue" (which is a "complete list"), dates back to the
seventeenth century. It has therefore an honourable history,
and it is a convenient single word with reference to a
list or **catalogue** that is drawn up. "The journal lists 80
societies concerned with this trade." It is now, however,
being used for, not making a list, but adding one or more
items to a list that is in existence, and it is an irresistible
attraction in journalese for avoiding such simple words as
include, mention, give. "Three new test players are listed in
the team selected to play against South Africa." "In the
report a number of factors are listed to explain why production is expected to have fallen short of the plan." "Suppose we are reduced to the ten countries listed above."
"Colin Thomas's *History of German Literature* fails to list
Stifter." At its worst we get such horrors as "In his application for a licence he listed his occupation as a director of a
well-known patent food company"; "A certain amount of
other accomplishment is listed by the author". Sometimes
the introduction of a new extension in the use of a word (as
well as slovenly syntax) is due to the search by journalists
for words that will fit into and show up in a headline:
"Minister lists more controls to relax".

locality does not mean place in an absolute sense, but (*a*) the exact spot, site, where something is to be found or has happened: "I wish I knew his present locality"; (*b*) the faculty of finding one's way in the phrase "sense of locality". It is incorrectly used for **place** absolutely, or **district**: e.g. in leaflets (trade term **brochures**) about hotels, holiday resorts, etc.: "This locality is dry and bracing".

LOOK, GAZE, PEER   **189**

look is the general working word. With this verb qualified by adverbs or adverbial phrases one can **look** at objects in different ways. **gaze**, however, without any qualification means to keep one's eyes fixed on an object, generally for some time: e.g. one **gazes** at a procession. To **peer** means to examine closely.

LUNCHEON, LUNCH   **190**

luncheon is a formal word (see 15). An Association will have an "annual luncheon"; a restaurant advertises and serves luncheons; but "Will you have lunch with me to-day?"

MAGICIAN, WIZARD, SORCERER, CONJURER,   **191**   ILLUSIONIST, JUGGLER

In most contexts **magician, wizard** (feminine, "witch"), and **sorcerer** are interchangeable, for persons who pretend to have supernatural or occult powers. **magician**, however, is used also as a close synonym of **conjurer** and **illusionist,** who practise mystifying tricks. A **juggler** is a **conjurer** whose tricks are confined to those of sleight-of-hand.

majority means "greater number or part": i.e. over half. Its proper use is restricted to that which can or theoretically could be counted. "A majority of the escaped prisoners were recaptured"; "A majority of my lettuce plants were killed by last night's frost"; but not "The majority (instead of **most**) of his work was scamped".

most also means more than half, and in some contexts the two words would be interchangeable. "A majority of the children have dinner at school." Although, however, there is no fixed point where **most** begins, it could hardly be used idiomatically if the numerical superiority were small. If, in a crate of apples, 51 per cent were rotten, a **majority** could be said to be so, but not **most**.

193 MALE, MASCULINE, MANLY, MANNISH, VIRILE

male (adjective) refers to the sex of a human being or animal: e.g. **male** servant, **male** leopard. It is used also with reference to flowers and plants, and to parts of machinery, e.g. **male** screw.

masculine in a roughly synonymous sense to that of **male** and the other words (i.e. apart from its use as a grammatical term) is restricted to human beings, and refers to qualities regarded as typical of man contrasted with woman. It can be applied to a woman having such qualities, physical or mental, rather than those typical of her own sex. Thus a woman might be said to have a **masculine** voice, or in a general sense a **masculine** character.

manly and **virile** refer to typical qualities in a man that are admirable, especially physical courage, forcefulness, outrightness.

mannish refers to qualities shown by a woman in outward ways, especially manner and clothes, that are affectedly **masculine**.

To the extent to which the distinction is observed, **malignant** and **malevolent** refer rather to intention or disposition, and are therefore restricted to persons; **malign** and **maleficent** refer to effect, and are not so restricted. Compare **benignant, benign; benevolent, beneficent** (16).

M.E.U. draws attention to a double inconsistency in medical language. Whereas one would expect that for a harmful growth the adjective would be **malign**, it is **malignant**. Contrariwise a harmless growth is not **benignant**, but **benign**. The use of **malignant** is perhaps due to a personifying tendency; and when these words were acquiring their medical sense the form **benignant** did not exist.

malicious is generally used with less weighty import than the other words, with reference to comparatively petty examples of ill-will, spite.

gentleman and **lady** show signs of becoming obsolete except in some stock phrases such as "Ladies and Gentlemen" at the opening of a speech; in shop jargon: e.g. "ladies' footwear"; in the notices, "Ladies," "Gentlemen," over the doors of lavatories. Otherwise the words tend to survive mainly as genteelisms (see 85) or snob-words (see 127) in the vocabulary of those who in the background of their minds are not sure that their own claims to class, culture, and money are unimpeachable. To say "At the party last evening I met an interesting lady who has just returned from Russia" would stamp one as genteel. The late Countess of Oxford and Asquith, on being asked to define a **lady**, answered "I have never met one". There is a story of another peeress, who, on returning to a shop to inquire about a purchase she had made, and being asked by a shop-walker "Do you remember if you were attended to by the gentleman over there with a black moustache?"

answered "No; by a nobleman with a bald head". Most of us are familiar with the epitaph in the memorial in the Antarctic, based on an entry in Scott's journal, to Captain Oates, who walked out into a blizzard to seek death in order to try to save his comrades: "Hereabouts died a very gallant gentleman". The account of this in Cherry-Garrard's *Worst Journey in the World* is beautiful and moving. Nevertheless linguistic taste and values change, and today a person would probably not use the word **gentleman**. **lady** dies more slowly than **gentleman**. Mr. Somerset Maugham mentions in *A Writer's Notebook* that outside lavatories one may see "Ladies" on one door but "Men" on the other. Some writers are unable to make up their mind whether female human beings are **ladies** or **women**. A recent article in *The Times* on swimming the Channel says that in Victoria's reign "only one man and no women swam it." Later on we are told that in the nineteen twenties and thirties "several ladies" did so.

196   MANNED, MANNED UP

manned up is one of the latest introductions into the language of a pleonastic combination of verb with a preposition of adverbial force. In a letter to *The Times*, for quotation from which the author and the publisher kindly give leave, Mr. Henry Strauss wrote: "Must industries be fully 'manned up' rather than 'manned'? Must the strong simple transitive verb, which is one of the main glories of our tongue, become obsolete in England as it appears to be in America? There (or at least in Hollywood) you never 'meet' a man: you 'meet up with' him; you never 'visit' friends: you 'visit with' them; you never 'study' a subject: you 'study up on' it." Mr. Strauss goes on to suggest that perhaps Sir Alan Herbert, after the manner in which he once rewrote Nelson's signal, will rewrite in the style of **manned up** etc. Mr. Winston Churchill's speech in January 1940: "Fill the armies, rule the air, pour out the munitions, strangle the U-boats, sweep the mines, plough the land, build the ships, guard the streets, succour the wounded, lift the downcast, and honour the brave".

For other usages where the combination of a verb with a preposition of adverbial force does not provide a meaning distinct from that given by the verb without this adjunct, or by some other well-established verb, compare **check up** (40), **face up to** (106).

Deprecation of these particular usages does not imply that all such combinations are bad. On the contrary in the development of the language such formations have introduced innumerable valuable additions to the vocabulary. We need think only of such common examples as **wash up, show off, give in, run down, fade away.** Thus "I must now go and wash up" means something different from "I must now go and wash"; **show off** implies a useful extension of the idea contained in **show** that is not so well provided for by any other word. Sir Alan Herbert, who is a watch-dog on the language, and never hesitates to attack fiercely any absurd inventions and extensions, says in *What a Word!* that some of those "adverbial particles", as he calls them, "do seem to have a magical and valuable power to enrich or distinguish a plebeian verb; and wherever they are properly employed to these ends we should be proud of them".

Our attitude to new usages, whether such formations or extensions of the use of established words, or new words, should be influenced chiefly by the answers that can be given to four questions about a candidate for admission to the language. (1) Does it provide a new meaning, even if the shade of distinction is fine? **manned up, face up, check up** are mere verbosity, but for recent combinations of verbs with prepositions of adverbial force that it is suggested may eventually become established with a distinctive sense see **step up** (345), **try out** (373), and **beat up** (366). (2) Does it enable a meaning to be expressed in a single word that hitherto has needed more than one? See **contact** (42), **humans** (143), **recondition** (284), **rehabilitate** (291), **service** (325). On the other hand, as Sir Alan Herbert points out in *What a Word!* the convenience of a single word could not be a good defence for such a clumsy one as "redecontamination". (3) Does the new use tend to obliterate an old use that has a distinctive and useful meaning? See **anticipate** (7), **aggravating** (169), **prejudice** (261), **protagonist** (272). (4) Is a new use so loose, so lacking in preciseness, that in a given context there is ambiguity about what is exactly meant? See **unthinkable** (381).

197 MANY, NUMEROUS

In most contexts the words would be interchangeable, but there is a distinction that would sometimes make one slightly more suitable than the other. **many** refers especially to a number of persons or things regarded collectively; **numerous** to their being regarded as occurring in succession. "Many displaced persons in Europe are unwilling to return to their own country." "I am filing this letter among numerous similar applications that have reached me from time to time."

At other times **numerous**, three-syllabled and Romance, is probably chosen, though unconsciously, in preference to the shorter Saxon **many** because **many** is used also as a noun or because its comparative length gives it an onomatopoeic effect; or for euphony: e.g. "They were not sufficiently numerous" sounds better than the jingle of "sufficiently many".

198 MAYBE, PERHAPS

Fowler in *M.E.U.* (1921) called **maybe** for **perhaps** a "stylish" word, with the warning that he was not using this adjective in a laudatory sense. The word, however, has now passed that stage, and must be regarded as established.

melody is often used as a synonym of **tune**, but a **melody** may not be a **tune**. Thus plainsong consists entirely of **melodies** that could not be called **tunes**. As Mr. Hubert Foss points out in *The Concertgoer's Handbook*, **tunes** are short and catchy, like, in verse, children's rhymes, whereas a **melody** may go on for a long time.

The adjective **melodious** is used as synonymous with **tuneful**. Here the user's right to the word in that sense there is none to dispute, for in the musical world also **melodious** might be so used, though probably with a somewhat derogatory implication, with reference to music that lacks serious, solid construction.

MEMORY, REMEMBRANCE, RECOLLECTION,   200
REMINISCENCE

memory can mean the general faculty, power, by which events, facts, etc., are kept in or brought back to the mind ("As one grows older one's memory declines"), but as a synonym of **remembrance, recollection, reminiscence** it refers to the events, etc., themselves as thought of.

recollection (="re-collecting", "bringing together again") generally implies a more deliberate, voluntary process than **remembrance,** for bringing back what has been out of mind. A common phrase is "in my recollection" rather than "in my remembrance".

remembrance, perhaps from its euphonious quality, is often used in solemn references: "There's rosemary, that's for remembrance"; "Remembrance Day."

reminiscence is generally used in the plural.

In the plural, **reminiscences** and **recollections** are used with reference to events, not only as thought and spoken of, but as related in writing; that is, as the subject matter of memoirs, autobiography.

For the verbs corresponding to these nouns see 293.

mental has for a long time been used in the phrases "mental patient", "mental home", "mental case", with reference to people of disordered mind. In recent years the adjective has come to be used either as an abbreviation for "mentally unstable", "mentally disordered;" or as a synonym of **neurotic**; or as a genteelism (see 34) by those shirking the words **mad** or **insane**. The precise meaning intended in a given context is often obscure, and the word in these senses is better avoided.

202   MENTALITY, MIND

mentality, which properly means "degree of intellectual power" (e.g. "Many grown-up people have the mentality of a child of ten"), has become a vogue-word (see 34), used loosely as a substitute for **mind, temperament, character, opinions, ideas, mental attitude** (e.g. "A broader mentality is needed towards this problem"). Like that of the adjective **mental** (see last article), its precise meaning in a given context is often obscure, and its use in these senses is to be avoided. The loose use of words with the suffix **-ality** often has a strong attraction for the woolly speaker and writer. Compare **personality** (244).

203 METICULOUS, SCRUPULOUS, PUNCTILIOUS, CAREFUL

meticulous is derived from the Latin *metus*="fear". The original sense was that of "fearful" (full of fear), "frightened". It is now a vogue-word (see 34) in a sense, taken from French usage, of **scrupulous, punctilious**, extremely or excessively **careful** about minute details.

minimize is derived from a Latin adjective in the superlative degree of comparison (*minimus*="smallest," "very small," "too small"). Correctly used it retains this superlative sense: concretely, "make as small as possible, or very small"; figuratively, "estimate to a very small, the smallest, an excessive degree," "belittle." "Several devices have been made to lessen the noise, but this is the one that will minimize it." "*Hamlet* in prose must always lose something, but André Gide's translation minimizes this loss." "In order to persuade them he minimized the difficulties." In an extension that loses the superlative sense it is often used, as an unnecessary substitute for established words, to mean merely **lessen, reduce**, and is sometimes absurdly qualified by an adverb of degree: e.g. a government department writes that a suggestion it makes should "minimize" the possibility of something "to a considerable extent".

MINUTE, SECOND, MOMENT, INSTANT   205

In their distinctive meanings, with reference to time, a **minute** is strictly one-sixtieth part of an hour, and a **second** one-sixtieth part of a minute; a **moment** is an extremely, but indefinitely, short time; an **instant** is a precise point of time: "I went that instant". All four words, however, are often used without distinction, especially colloquially, in the sense of **moment**, as above. "I shall not be a moment (or minute, or second, or instant)."

MISHAP, ACCIDENT   206

An **accident** (Latin *accidere*="to fall out") is primarily an event happening by chance. "By accident" means "by chance", "by an unintentional act". There can be a "happy accident;" generally, however, the word implies an undesirable event. **mishap** ("unfortunate happening") is generally restricted to an undesirable event that, compared with the common use of **accident**, is not serious. To run over a person with a motor-car is an **accident**; to have a puncture, and be prevented from arriving punctually for an appointment, is a **mishap**.

207   MISS, LOSE

In some contexts these words, in the sense of fail to do something, could be interchanged. You can **miss** or **lose** a train. Where a distinction is recognizable, **lose** is the word generally used for a failure that is permanent, final. A tennis-player **misses** a stroke, but he **loses** a game.

208   MISTAKE, ERROR, FALLACY

Every **fallacy** involves a **mistake** or **error**, but all **mistakes** and **errors** are not **fallacies**. **fallacy** is strictly a word in logic for an argument violating the laws of correct reasoning. Outside this technical use its meaning ought to be confined to that of a "misleading argument," but it is often used as a substitute for **mistake** or **error**. To say that Tennyson died before Browning is a **mistake** or **error**. Before the time of Galileo the sun was thought to revolve round the earth: that was a **mistake** or **error**. Neither was a **fallacy**.

For **mistake** and **error** see also 337.

209   MODERATE, MEDIOCRE, MODEST

moderate and **modest** are derived from the Latin *moderatus* and *modestus*, which in their turn are based on the word *modus* in its sense of bounds, limit, restriction. **mediocre** is derived from the Latin *medius*="middle", "intermediate". The three words are synonymous as epithets for something half-way between good and bad, great and small, etc.: e.g. "a man of moderate (or mediocre or modest) ability or attainments". **moderate** and **mediocre** are more common than **modest** in this sense. **mediocre** generally has a depreciatory implication: "a mediocre play". With reference to price, fee, demand, etc., **moderate** implies what is reasonable, not high or exorbitant; **modest** what is so small that, even if it were somewhat larger, it would still fall well within the limits of what would be **moderate. mediocre** is not used in this sense.

The words are sometimes qualified by adverbs of superlative degree. As their essential idea is of something between extremes, "very", "most", "extremely", etc., are not by strict logic applicable. Language, however, is not always logical, and "His charges are very (or most) moderate (or modest)" would be idiomatic, and even "Her knowledge of French is very mediocre".

For **modest** in another sense see next article.

MODEST, DIFFIDENT, SHY 210

For **modest**=**moderate, mediocre,** see last article. **modest** in another sense could in some contexts be roughly synonymous with **diffident** and **shy** with reference to a person who has a humble estimate of his merits or capacities. Generally, however, **diffident** implies lack of self-confidence, especially in being hesitant over taking action in given circumstances: "He was **diffident** about raising the point just then"; and **shy**, timidity in manner, anxiety to avoid observation. A person who is **modest** in his opinion of himself is not necessarily **diffident** about taking action or **shy** in expressing himself; and a person who is neither **modest** nor **diffident** can in his manner be embarrassingly **shy**.

MOTIVATE, ACTIVATE, ACTUATE 211

actuate means primarily "communicate motion to" a machine; thence, with the sense of acting upon the will, it came to be used for "serve as a motive to", "influence", conduct. "I am sure this offer was actuated by a sincere desire to help." The word is well established in this sense.

activate, which means primarily "make active"—especially in physics, "make radio-active"—has become extended recently to mean the same as **actuate** in the sentence given above. "He said that these suggestions for the improvement of the track had been activated by considerations of safety." **motivate**, which is used in the same sense, is an entirely new word. "Many of those deserters were motivated not by cowardice but by domestic anxieties." Neither **motivate** nor **activate** is a helpful addition to the language.

212   MUTUAL, COMMON, RECIPROCAL

mutual implies, with reference to two or more people, that A does or stands to B as B does or stands to A, or that more than two people do or stand to each other in this way. If A gives B help, and B gives A help, they give each other **mutual** help. If A is a well-wisher of B, and B is of A, they are **mutual** well-wishers. Similarly, if A, B and C have the same relations to each other in these matters, the relation is **mutual**. "The three sections of the party were divided by mutual suspicions and jealousies."

common implies not the relation of two or more persons with reference to what they do or stand to each other, but their relation to some other person or thing. If A and B are both interested in flying, flying is a **common** interest. If A and B both fear C, the fear of him is **common** to them. If A and B are friends of D, D is a **common** friend of theirs.

The use of **mutual** in the sense of **common** goes back to the end of the sixteenth century, but has for long been regarded as improper. The title given by Dickens to his novel *Our Mutual Friend* encouraged this use, which moreover in spite of grammarians is sometimes found among good writers. I am indebted to Mr. E. M. Forster for the following comments. "I am slightly prejudiced in favour of 'mutual'. Common, bears also the sense of vulgar, and there are times when one does not want even the hint of that sense to creep in." In consideration of this opinion, and from such a high quarter, we ought perhaps to accept the use as established—and on more cogent grounds than two other Dickensian uses, **aggravating** and **phenomenon** (see 169 and 249).

reciprocal can be used as a synonym of **mutual**, but it can refer also to the state or action of only one of two persons to the other. If in the spring A has helped B in his garden, and in the summer B helps A in his, B is giving A **reciprocal** help.

MYTH, LEGEND, FABLE, PARABLE, 213
ALLEGORY

In its roughly synonymous relation to the other words a **myth** is a traditional story, usually involving supernatural beings, that attempts an explanation of some natural phenomenon: e.g. the story of Proserpine's spending half the year in Hades with Pluto, and half on earth, as explaining the cause of spring and winter, or as symbolical of the seed in the ground and the growth of the corn. (In its common colloquial use a **myth** is a story that purports to be true and is not, or an attempt at explanation that fails to explain.)

A **legend** is a traditional story popularly regarded as historical: e.g. of Romulus and Remus, King Alfred and the cakes, the founding of Glastonbury Abbey by Joseph of Arimathea.

A **fable** is sometimes used as synonymous with **myth,** but more often it means a story made up to draw a lesson: e.g. the **fables** of Aesop and La Fontaine, which deal with human virtues and vices under the guise of animal behaviour. In this sense its meaning is closely allied to that of **parable**, in which the lesson drawn is restricted to moral or spiritual relations.

An **allegory** is a narrative description of a subject under guise of another suggestively similar (*C.O.D.*): e.g. Bunyan's *Pilgrim's Progress*.

From another aspect Dean Inge in *Mysticism in Religion* treats **fable** and **myth** as contrasted with **allegory**. "In **allegory** the thought is grasped first and then arranged in a particular dress. In the **myth** thought and form come into being together; the thought is the vital principle which shapes the form; the form is the sensible image which displays the thought. The **parable** is distinct from both. In the Gospels the Sower is an **allegory**, the Prodigal Son a **parable**, and Sheep and Goats a **myth**."

214   NEAR, NEAR-BY, NEIGHBOURING, NIGH

near-by (often spelt **nearby**), primarily an adverb, shows signs of becoming established adjectivally as a synonym of **near, neighbouring**. "Before breakfast we always climbed a near-by hill." As Sir Alan Herbert points out, there is an analogy of this use in **far-off**, which, originally an adverb, is now established as also an adjective: e.g. "old, unhappy, far-off things" (Wordsworth). **nigh** is archaic, but like many other archaisms is a fairly frequent affectation of journalese for **near**, as an adjective, adverb, and preposition.

215   NEED, WANT, REQUIRE, DEMAND

(1) **need, want**, and (on the formal side: see 15) **require** are synonymous in the sense of "ought to have", "deserve". "The bracket wants (or needs or requires) an extra screw." "That boy wants (or needs or requires) a whipping."

(2) **want**, however, has also the meaning of "desire", "wish". A tramp may **need** or **require** a bath, but, so far from **wanting** one, in this sense, may be averse from having it when it is offered to him. On the other hand a man who has already drunk more than is good for him does not **need** or **require** another drink, but may **want** it. A statesman said that a good government gives the citizens what they **need**, and not what they **want**.

(3) There is a use of **require** with the meaning of "insist".

"The Headmaster requires of all pupils obedience to the laws of the School."

demand can be synonymous with (3), as e.g. in the last sentence; and with (1): "This letter demands an immediate answer"; "The work was monotonous but demanded concentration"; but in these senses is on the formal side.

The uses of the nouns **need, want, requirement, demand** correspond with those of the verbs.

For **demand** in another sense see 161.

exigence and (more common) **exigency**, both generally in the plural, are used to express a **need** that is extremely urgent.

Euphony, operating knowingly or unknowingly, is an element in language often determining in a given context the choice between words that are synonymous, even when in other circumstances one might be preferable to another. Thus, though **require** has been classed above as on the formal side, the phrase **the number required** might be preferred to **the number needed** (with the two n's and two d's).

NEVER, NOT   216

Strictly, **never** refers to something that has not happened, is not happening, or will not happen, over a period of time. "From youth to middle age I hoped to get to Switzerland for winter sports, but I never had enough money;" "However long you argue you will never convince him". It is often, however, used merely as an emphatic **not**: "When I used that word I never intended to be offensive".

NICE, PLEASANT   217

nice, which in the sense of "precise", "subtle", goes back several centuries, still has its valuable use in such phrases as "a nice point". Today its common use is as a synonym for a multitude of adjectives that imply some form of "pleasantness". The matter could not be put better than it is in

Treble and Vallins's *ABC of English Usage.* "The worst
that can be said for **nice** in this usage is that it is nearly
always vapid, and therefore to be avoided in serious writing;
and the best, that it is a convenient stand-by, though a great
encourager of laziness, in conversation. It is difficult to
imagine what we should do without **nice** in, for example,
our comments on the weather; but when we go back a little
and find Gilbert White speaking not tamely of a **nice** but
lyrically of a **sweet** day, or Shakespeare and Milton with
their vast range of adjectives for wind and weather, we begin
to realize what we have lost in sacrificing our birthright in
epithets for the paltry gift of so insignificant a word."

218   NIL, NOTHING

nil is used chiefly in scoring at games: e.g. "three goals to
nil," or is a formal word (see 15) in statistical reports, etc.:
e.g. in "nil returns" on an income tax sheet. Otherwise it is
an affectation of journalese.

219   NOSTALGIA, YEARNING

nostalgia (Greek *nostos*="return home," *algos*="pain"),
originally meant an aching longing for home, **home-
sickness**. It is now used widely with reference, not to heart-
ache for home, but to other kinds of intense **yearning**,
especially for the past. As has been pointed out in the
article on **hectic** (see 138), no satisfactory reason can be
given for objecting on principle to the extension of the use
of words from their original sense. But **nostalgia**, together
with the adjective **nostalgic** and the adverb **nostalgically**, has
become a wearisome vogue-word (see 34).

> One word far more than most gives me neuralgia,
> And that's nostalgic, and its mate nostalgia.
> I own the word itself's nostalgic, very:
> It's sick for home within the dictionary.

(Quoted with the permission of the Proprietors of *Punch*.)

number, for **song** and dance **tune** ("dance number") is jargon used by leaders of bands at restaurants, dance halls, and the like. A musical publisher, too, will sometimes advertise "the latest numbers".

OBJECT, DEMUR 221

Both words mean "be in opposition to", "in disagreement with". The chief distinctions are that **object** can imply that the opposition or disagreement is in thought or in word, whereas **demur** always implies that it is expressed in word; and that a person **objecting** in word may do so strongly, even violently, whereas **demur** implies a quiet, polite, orderly manner.

OBLIVIOUS, FORGETFUL, UNMINDFUL 222

forgetful is the general working word for "not having memory", "losing memory".

unmindful means, not so much failure of memory (which may sometimes be, though a defect, not seriously culpable), as culpably "taking no thought of", "paying no attention to", some person or thing. It generally has the implication that duty, wisdom, etc., should have caused one to give thought or attention to a matter: e.g. that one has been **unmindful** of the rights of others.

oblivious can be synonymous with **forgetful** and **unmindful**, often with the sense that one fails to remember through being preoccupied. It is often used loosely, however, as synonymous with "indifferent", "unaware", "unconscious", "inattentive": e.g. "oblivious of the danger" (="blind to", or "ignorant of" it). The nearest it can correctly get to these meanings is in the sense of "no longer aware".

223 OBTAIN, PROCURE, SECURE, ACQUIRE, GAIN, WIN, GET

In the roughly synonymous senses of these words **get** is the ordinary working one. **obtain, procure, secure, acquire** are generally formal (see 15) or genteelisms (see 85) or commercialese. Shopkeepers and other salesmen like to **obtain** or **procure** rather than to **get,** without meaning anything more. In some contexts, however, the four words can imply, more than **get** would, the coming into possession of a thing with some effort.

If the ubiquitous **get** is disliked, it can often be replaced by some more definite word, e.g. **buy.**

gain and **win** are generally restricted to the idea of **getting** something desirable, but are sometimes used in a satirical sense: "He gained (or won) a reputation for duplicity".

In an intransitive use **obtain,** meaning **prevail, exist, be in force, be in vogue, have place, subsist,** goes back to the early seventeenth century. Swift so used it: "This, though it failed at present, afterwards obtained". Today, however, it smacks of journalese.

The adjectives **obtainable** and **procurable** are not formal but ordinary working words. Recently, however, they have been superseded by **available.**

224 OCCIDENT, WEST; ORIENT, EAST

C.O.D. gives **Occident** and **Orient** as "poetical, rhetorical," and for ordinary purposes they would hardly appear except in journalese.

225 OFTEN, FREQUENTLY

In the sense of merely "many times", **frequently,** three-syllabled and romance, instead of its shorter Saxon synonym **often,** is on the formal side (see 15), though a tendency to use it is probably influenced by its having a corresponding adjective, **frequent,** whereas **often** has not. **frequently,** in a fine distinction, is more suitable when deliberate, habitual action by human beings is concerned. "She frequently sends him money", "Business frequently brings him to London"; but "I often ran across him in those days", "Frosts often occur as late as May".

OLD, ELDERLY, SENESCENT, AGED, ANCIENT, 226
VETERAN, SENILE, ANTIQUATED

The general word for meaning "advanced in age" is **old**. It can apply to persons or things. **elderly, veteran** and **senile** refer to persons only; **aged** (rather formal: see 15) to persons or living things; **ancient** usually only to things, though there is Coleridge's poem, *The Ancient Mariner*, and we call the civilized nations of antiquity, the Greeks and the Romans, the **Ancients.**

elderly and (not often used) **senescent** mean "growing old".

ancient refers to times long past, "especially before the fall of the Western Roman Empire" (*C.O.D.*): e.g. with reference to a "custom", "monument", "civilization".

veteran usually refers to persons that have grown old in experience: "veteran troops", "veteran golfer", "veteran statesman".

senile is used of a person who shows the feebleness of old age.

antiquated refers to a person who is out of date, or to an object, idea, custom, etc., that is obsolescent.

ONSLAUGHT, ASSAULT, ATTACK   227

Both in a military sense and figuratively an **onslaught** is an **attack** that is sudden, concentrated, violent. **assault** militarily is generally restricted to an **attack** on the walls of a fortress; non-militarily, [fortress; non-militarily, to a legal sense.]

hopeful means "having hope": not necessarily, in spite of the suffix -ful, "full of hope": "I am still hopeful that he will come" could mean "I still have some, though not much, hope".

sanguine, meaning "having a high degree of hope", is not much used.

optimistic (Latin *optimus*="best") and the nouns **optimism** and **optimist** have primarily a grave and philosophical meaning with reference to the doctrine of the ascendancy in the world of good over evil, as contrasted with the opposite doctrine of **pessimism**. The words have come to be applied, however, to the hope or strong belief that events, schemes, etc., will turn out favourably. Thus with reference to a large matter a person might be said to be **optimistic** that difficulties in an international situation would be solved without recourse to war. Similarly in a small matter a person might be said to be **optimistic** that a cricket team would be able at all events to bring about a draw; his acquaintances might call him an **optimist** for believing this; if it did happen, he might say that his **optimism** had been justified. Fowler nearly thirty years ago deplored this use as a "modern popular triviality". but it continues to be so widespread that it must be regarded as firmly established. The words are, however, so overworked: e.g. "The Soviet delegate raised some optimism by his readiness to discuss this subject," that it would be refreshing to find at all events **hopeful**, **hope, hopefulness**, restored to the vocabulary, even though there is no single word to correspond to **optimist**. Moreover in their popular use the words tend to lose connection with their derivation from a superlative adjective (Latin *optimus*=best), and speakers and writers use such phrases as "very optimistic", "strong optimism", "a great optimist". (See also **optimistic**, 248.)

order is the usual working word. It is often used in the plural even when only one thing is to be done or not done, and this is stated only once. "His orders were to return next day" is as idiomatic as "His order was . . ."

command is rare except in military language.

instruction is generally used in the plural, even when, as with **orders**, the reference is only to one statement and to one thing to be done or not done.

direction, in a similar sense, but less common, is always used in the plural.

directive appears in the Oxford dictionaries only as an adjective. It has recently come to be used as a noun, and as synonymous with **order**, etc., especially with reference to official matters of high policy. Mr. Winston Churchill in *The Second World War* writes of "the series of his directives . . . upon the daily conduct of the war".

injunction is a formal word (see 15) for **order**, etc., but sometimes means only authoritative advice. (It has also a legal sense for judicial compulsion to do, or restrain from doing, something.)

The corresponding verbs are **order, command, instruct, direct**, and (colloquially in the legal sense) **injunct**. For informal use **tell** is the common word.

ORNAMENTAL, ORNATE, DECORATIVE   230

ornamental refers to that which decorates (active). "Strip an Italian chapel of the fifteenth century of its ornamental adjuncts, and an uninteresting shell is left" (J. A. Symonds). **ornate** refers to that which is decorated (passive), generally with the sense of decoration that is elaborate, and often with the implication of excessive decoration. We may contrast the plain style of one orator with the style of another that is **ornate** with images, etc. It is the images he uses that are **ornamental**.

otherwise is an adverb, meaning "in another way". Consequently the phrase **or otherwise** is admissible only if the alternative to which **otherwise** refers is either an adverb or an adverbial phrase. (1) "It is too early yet to form an opinion whether the plan will work satisfactorily or otherwise." Similarly with **and otherwise**. (2) "He made several further attempts to get into touch with her both by direct approach and otherwise." The phrases are used incorrectly when **otherwise** is made to serve as a correlative to a noun, adjective, or verb, often as a substitute for **not**. (3) "I cannot tell whether the plan will be a success or otherwise" (**otherwise** should be **not** or a **failure**). (4) "It is still too early to know whether the plan will work or otherwise." (**otherwise** should be **not** or **fail**). (5) "They made no further threats, economic or otherwise" (**otherwise** should be **other** or **political, military,** etc.). Three recent examples come from high circles: from an eminent lawyer, "I did not think it proper to form any judgment on the truth or otherwise of the reports"; from a learned association, "The Council invite —— to substantiate or otherwise the statements"; from a Professor of English Literature in an article entitled "Arnold and Pater: Critics Historical, Aesthetic and Otherwise".

It will be noticed that even when **or otherwise** is used correctly as in (1) it is redundant; and even with the suggested alterations in (3) and (4) any words after **success** and **work** are redundant.

232   OVERALL, TOTAL, WHOLE

Until recently **overall** as a noun has been used only for a garment "over everything" (compare "overcoat"="coat worn over another coat"): e.g. a woman's loose work-garment; in the plural, a man's trousers, leggings, outer suit for dirty work or bad weather. "The coupon equivalent will be made out for 'operating gowns' or 'industrial coat

overalls' " (Clothing Regulations). On the other hand **over-all** (with a hyphen) has been used adjectivally, meaning "inclusive of everything between the extreme ends": e.g. "a cruiser with an over-all length of 335 feet." In an extension of this adjectival use, but generally spelt, like the noun, without a hyphen, **overall** has become a vogue-word (see 34) as a synonym of **total**, **whole** (adjectives), which, as Mr. Ivor Brown points out, are seldom seen in journalism nowadays. "The overall output was x tons." "The joint framework for defence to be set up will be overall and elastic." "We must be persuaded that Russia had abandoned her overall objective."

In these uses the adjective is at best an inelegant variation. It may sometimes, however, be convenient for combining in a single word the idea of "supreme", "at the top", with that of "complete", "comprehensive". "Admittedly the overall direction of this British communistic movement came from the Kremlin."

PACT, COMPACT 233

As a rule **pact** is used for an agreement between nations or large bodies of people; **compact** for an arrangement between private persons.

PAINFUL, POIGNANT 234

poignant (Latin *pungere*="to prick" or "sting") is the stronger of the two words, implying pain that is acute. Both words apply to physical or mental pain, but **poignant** more usually to the latter.

PAINTER, ARTIST, ARTISTE 235

A **painter** is (*a*) one who puts paint on walls, ships' sides, etc.; (*b*) one who paints pictures. A **painter** of pictures would not usually speak of himself or another of his craft as an **artist**, thereby implicitly claiming a monopoly for his profession of a word that includes also writers, musicians, sculptors, etc. **artist** used for one who practices the profession of painting is a genteelism. A **painter** of pictures may or may not be an **artist**. On the other hand one might praise a talented artisan for using paint with "the touch of an artist." There are perhaps contexts in which **artist** is convenient for particular reference to practisers of the visual arts apart from painting: e.g. draughtsmen, sculptors, engravers, architects. (The Royal Academy of Arts is for painting, drawing, and sculpture.) "Many were surprised, though pleased, when the Proprietors of *Punch* appointed as editor an artist" (i.e. not a writer). Similarly "An artist in black and white" is a description of Aubrey Beardsley. Nevertheless if a child asked "Who (or what) was Rembrandt?" the answer should be "A painter," and not "An artist". (See also p. 198).

artiste is a journalistic or professional word for a performer on the stage, male or female, in singing, dancing, etc.

236   PART, PORTION, SHARE, PROPORTION, PERCENTAGE

part is the working word. "Part of the cake was insufficiently baked." "The lower part of the garden was given over to an aviary."

portion, which in these examples would have been a genteelism (see 85), should be restricted to the sense of a **share**. "That is your portion of the cake." "My portion of the profit was £1,000." "Brief life is here our portion" (the share of eternity granted to human beings by God).

proportion, for **part**, **number**, **many**, etc., is a show-word (see 15), presumably favoured for its mathematical air and its length. It should be restricted to uses where a ratio is stated or implied. *M.E.U.* gives as an example of correct use: "We hope to pass next year a greater proportion of candidates" (i.e. a **number**, related to the total entry, that will be greater than the corresponding number this year);

of incorrect use: "A greater proportion of the candidates passed" (with **proportion** here used incorrectly, instead of e.g. "the greater part" or "most" or "a large majority"). Similarly incorrect: "Of the 1,000 resignations of officers from the Army in the last eighteen months a considerable proportion is due to the difficulty the young married officer has in living on his service pay." "A proportion of the men at West India Docks are out on strike." The word is perhaps justifiable or even desirable in such a sentence as "Of the multitude of books published every year only a small proportion are profitable". The total, absolute, number here is so large (e.g. in 1950 in this country it was more than 16,000) that a profitable minority of even only one in twenty would come to 800, and "a small number", unless qualified by "comparatively" or "relatively", might give a misleading impression.

percentage is another word, derived from mathematics, favoured by the sham erudite. Its use should be restricted to numerical statements: e.g. "The percentage of successful candidates was 65". There is no point in saying that "a large percentage of the apples arrived bruised", instead of "a large part" or "a large number" or "many".

Similarly **per cent,** especially a **hundred per cent,** is over-worked by being used when simpler means of expression are available. Thus we read "Nearly a hundred per cent [instead of "all"] apple trees have suffered injury in the recent frost"; "The production of the firm has gone up a hundred per cent" [instead of "doubled"]; "Mills are now running at a hundred per cent [instead of "full"] capacity"; "Requirements have been met a hundred per cent" [instead of "fully" or "completely"]; and worse still, "The experiment has been a hundred per cent [instead of "complete" or "entire"] success". Similarly with **fifty per cent,** where "half" could be used; **twenty-five per cent** for "a quarter": **ten per cent** for "a tenth", etc. For some proportions, however, the usage can be convenient. **forty per cent** (or

40%) is simpler than "four out of ten", 30% than "three out of ten". Nevertheless enumeration by percentages is better avoided, if possible, as striking too statistical a note, except in scientific or technical subject matter. This some years ago was borne in on me by my friend J. C. Smith. I had written an essay on the poetry of Hardy, in which, referring to his poems on love, I compared the greater frequency of that theme in his *Collected Poems* than in Palgrave's *Golden Treasury*, and I expressed this in percentages. Smith, on reading the proofs, questioned my phrasing, which I thereupon altered so as to remove the offending **percentages**.

237   PARTAKE, PARTICIPATE, SHARE

partake for the single word **share** or the phrase **take part** is journalese. It has also a special genteel use with reference to food: 'They invited us to partake of the meal"; or—as a synonym of merely **eat**—"Being ravenously hungry after the long walk I partook with gusto of my packet of sandwiches".

participate as a synonym of **share** or **take part** is on the formal side (see 15). The nouns, however, **participator**, **participant**, **participation**, would be in many contexts more idiomatic than **share** (or **sharing**) and **sharer**.

238   PASS, DIE, EXPIRE, DECEASE, PERISH ; PASSING, DEATH, DECEASE, DEMISE

Verbs

die is the ordinary working word. **pass away, pass hence, pass over, pass from among us,** are genteelisms (see 85). Living creatures do not today **expire**, except in journalese, though treaties, strike notices, and other arrangements with a time limit do. **decease** and **demise** are legal words. **perish** refers to widespread destruction: e.g. massacre or a cataclysm of nature.

Nouns

passing is a genteelism. **decease, deceased** (noun and adjective), and **demise** are legal words.

PECUNIARY, MONETARY, FINANCIAL 239

pecuniary is a show-word (see 15) for **monetary**. "He was in pecuniary [instead of **monetary, financial**, or **money**] difficulties."

PEOPLE, PERSONS, FOLK 240

When one is referring to more than one **person**, in the sense of men and women in general, the plural **persons** is less commonly used—one might almost say less idiomatic— than **people** (as a plural noun). "At the party I met several people who knew you." "There were thousands of people in the park." **persons**, however, has since the last war come into frequent use in the term "displaced persons". **folk** is affected or archaic, except in a few compound words or phrases: "folklore", "folksong", "the old folk at home", "the women folk".

PERMISSION, CONSENT, LEAVE, PERMIT 241

leave is the ordinary working word. The use of **permission** would be on the formal side (see 15) except with reference to circumstances and conditions that themselves are formal: e.g. official and legal regulations. **consent** is generally restricted to the giving of **leave** that has been asked for. **permit** is **leave** expressed in a written order, certificate, etc.

The use of the verbs **permit** and **consent** corresponds to that of their nouns as given in the last article. The verbs that serve for the sense of the noun **leave** are **let** and **allow**. For adjectival constructions the past participle of **permit** is used. "The holder of a certificate to a club for sales in special hours must exhibit a notice stating the **permitted** hours."

243   PERPETRATE, COMMIT

Both words are used in a bad sense, with reference to a crime or blunder. **perpetrate** is a show-word (see 15) or is used facetiously: e.g. "perpetrating a joke", "perpetrating a poem".

244   PERSONALITY:
(1) PERSON, PERSONAGE, PARTY;
(2) INDIVIDUALITY, CHARACTER, DISPOSITION TEMPERAMENT

personality is primarily someone's existence or identity.

(1) It is often misused, by hankerers after long words, for person. "The appointment of Mr. Morrison to be Mr. Bevin's successor at the Foreign Office is a change of personalities involving no change of policy."

(1) A **personage** is someone of rank or importance. This word too is often misused for **person**. "He is a strange personage."

party for **person**, unless used with reference to two or more people entering into an agreement, or making the two sides in a legal action, is facetious.

(2) **personality** can perhaps sometimes serve a useful purpose for the meaning of **individuality** marked by strong external traits in bearing, manner, etc. "While technically his dancing is good, he lacks personality." It has become, however, a wearisomely overworked vogue-word (see 34), as a substitute for **character**, **disposition**, **temperament**. "He

has a complicated personality." "Goebbels's personality is not in the least interesting." "The keynote of her personality was charity." In many contexts the precise meaning is obscure, and for the word to be given a long and entire rest would be a blessed relief. Compare **mentality** (202).

personality, generally in the plural, has a distinctive meaning, of a remark in a spoken or written statement about someone, especially of an offensive sort, or about private matters that are not relevant to the point at issue.

PERSONALLY, MYSELF   **245**

personally is today used mostly as merely an emphasizer, which has displaced the now comparatively rare use, in this way, of **myself**, and in this sense it is generally pleonastic. "There are some who enjoy motoring—independently of its practical convenience for some purposes—as a pastime. I personally dislike it." "If you ask my advice about the investment, personally I would not touch it." "To many people the scenery of mountainous country has the greatest appeal; personally I prefer softly rolling country or even the flatness of Holland." Take the last sentence: the juxtaposition of "many people" and "I" provides adequate contrast; or why not, instead of **personally**, simply **but**? At the best **personally** in this sense is much overworked, and the word should generally be reserved for use with something that might in other circumstances be non-personal. "The Minister went personally into all the figures": he might have delegated this work to a subordinate. "I am known to him personally": I might be known to him only by name, reputation, etc. "As Secretary I shall have to carry out the Committee's decision, though personally I disapprove of it."

PERSONNEL, STAFF, EMPLOYEE, WORKER   246

personnel (from the French), for **staff, employees, workers,** etc., is a recent vogue-word (see 34). "Two hundred naval personnel of the visiting destroyers in Glasgow will each give a pint of blood to the Blood Transfusion Service." Presumably the journalist who wrote this thought "Two hundred of the crew" too simple and mean. "A large personnel was housed in this building." "We kept 400 personnel in North Russia to handle our convoys." A government regulation, quoted by Sir Alan Herbert, mentions "Personnel who have lost the sight of one eye". A recent article in *The Times* said: "That this word should be classed as vermin few sensible people will deny. Like the grey squirrel it ought never to have been imported: it is a pest to be eliminated". To do this would need first the lopping off of the top branches of some official trees where it gaily romps. Thus there is at the Admiralty a "Chief of Naval Personnel".

247   PERUSE, READ

peruse is sometimes used to imply that thoroughness and care are given to the **reading** of something: e.g. a legal document before signing it. Otherwise it is a show-word of the kind dear to the heart of the sham-erudite (see 15).

248   PESSIMISTIC, HOPELESS

The same considerations that apply to the popular use of **optimistic, optimist, optimism** (see 228) apply to the use of **pessimistic, pessimist, pessimism**, with reference to a belief that something will turn out unfavourably.

Perhaps the displacement of **hopeless** by **pessimistic** in even trivial contexts is due partly to the fact that **hopeless**, besides its meaning with reference to a person who feels no hope, has a secondary meaning, with reference to a thing or person that is beyond hope of betterment. "The situation is hopeless"; "He is a hopeless liar".

In its strict meaning a **phenomenon** is a thing that appears or is perceived or observed. It is applied chiefly to a fact or occurrence the cause of which is in question; philosophically to that of which the senses or the mind directly takes note: an immediate object of perception—the opposite of **noumenon,** which is an object of intellectual intuition. "Her empirical study occasionally gives way to intuition or superstition, but I think her analysis of natural phenomena is on the whole sound." In an extended sense the word came to be used for a highly exceptional or unaccountable fact or occurrence, a **prodigy.** Dickens contributed to this popularity by his phrase "infant phenomenon". It is true that a **prodigy** may be a **phenomenon** in the strict sense of that word, but a **phenomenon** is not necessarily a **prodigy, exception, unusual occurrence, remarkable circumstance,** etc.: "A phenomenon connected with change of temperature in water is the formation of ice". Thirty years ago Fowler thought that the adjective from **phenomenon—phenomenal—**having passed through the stage of being a vogue-word (see 34), as a synonym of **prodigious, exceptional, unusual, remarkable, extraordinary,** etc., had fallen into discredit, and he hoped it would soon die unregretted. It still, however, survives and flourishes in these senses. *C.O.D.* enters the extended meaning of **phenomenon** without any derogatory comment of "colloquial" or "vulgar"; and Sir Ernest Gowers in *Plain Words* says—too tolerantly, some will consider—that, as this use has the "unimpeachable authority" of Professor Weekley, it may be considered within sight of becoming established: presumably also **phenomenal,** and the adverb **phenomenally.**

PITIFUL, PITEOUS, PITIABLE 250

piteous as used now—but the word is nearly obsolete—refers to a person who feels pity, who is "compassionate".

pitiful can refer both to a person who feels pity, and to a person or thing rousing pity. **pitiable** is restricted to a person or thing rousing pity. **pitiful** (in the sense of rousing pity) and **pitiable** often today imply pity mixed largely with contempt.

251   PLACE, PUT

place has some special idiomatic uses. "I can't place him"="I can't get him into the right place in my memory." "Gordon Richards' horse was not placed (or was unplaced) in the 3.30 race." Otherwise **place**, as a synonym for **put**, is a genteelism (see 85).

252   PLAN, SCHEME, BLUE-PRINT

blue-print has become in recent years familiar jargon for **plan, scheme**. "The United Nations General Assembly has adopted the blue-print for the settlement of the Korean crisis prepared by Britain and seven other countries." The *Oxford English Dictionary* defines blue-print as "a photo-print composed of white lines on a blue ground, used chiefly in copying plans, etc." That is to say, the essential meaning of a **blue-print** in its literal sense is that it is a copy of a drawn plan. To use this highly technical word in a figurative sense as a substitute for the simple and established words **plan** and **scheme** is therefore a perverse as well as a super-fluous extension.

253   POLISH, BURNISH

Both words are defined in dictionaries as "make smooth and glossy by friction"; but in common usage **polish** is the general word, and **burnish** is used only with reference to metals.

courteous has a stronger sense than **polite**. **polite** often has only a negative implication, with reference to action or words that are the reverse of rough, peremptory, rude, whereas **courteous** implies that the action or words exceed in thoughtful consideration and gracious form the demands of mere **politeness**. The same shade of difference is shown in the nouns **politeness** and **courtesy**.

POLITIC, EXPEDIENT   255

Both words refer to action that is prudent and is taken because it is advantageous. In their classic use the **expedient** course looks to the end, the **politic** to the means. **expedient**, however, has come to imply a course that, though prudent and for that reason desirable, is not ideally the best: "Too fond of the right to pursue the expedient" (Goldsmith).

POSSESSION, ADVANTAGE, ASSET   256

asset has become established popularly as a singular word, with plural **assets**. Strictly **assets** (from the French *assez*= enough) is a singular noun ending in *s*, meaning that which is enough to meet liabilities. (Legally the singular form **asset** is not recognized.) "In the bankruptcy proceedings his liabilities were estimated as about £10,000 and his assets about £3,000." "Today many landowners have large gardens that owing to increasing costs of maintenance are fast becoming more of a liability than an asset." In loose extensions **asset** and **assets** have become vogue-words (see 34) as synonyms of a large number of simple and established words such as **possession**, **advantage**, **gain**, **benefit**, or even **quality** and **cause**. Thus we are told that a tennis player's "most useful asset is his strong drive". "Club practice is a handy asset to doctors." "Its marvellous air is an asset of Brighton's popularity." "Through all his troubles he had the assets of good health and an adequate income."

possible has two main meanings: (a) "able to be", covering also the idea of "able to happen"; (b) "able to be done", covering also the idea of "able to be carried out".

feasible has meaning (b) but not (a). It is, however, often misused, to mean (a). "As a thunderstorm seemed feasible [should be "possible"] we decided to turn back." "With reasonable care it would have been feasible [should be "practicable"] to avoid the accident." In other misuses it stands for **probable, manageable, convenient, serviceable, plausible,** etc.

practical (when it refers to things) and **practicable** come near to each other in sense. *M.E.U.* points out that, though **practicable** means capable of being effected or accomplished, in sense (b) of **possible** (see above), and **practical** means adapted to certain conditions, it is true that the **practicable** is often **practical**, and the **practical** nearly always **practicable**; but that a **practical** plan may prove owing to circumstances **impracticable**, and a **practicable** policy may be **unpractical.**.

practical, with reference to persons, means one who, not concerned with principles or theories, gets things done. **practicable** is not applied to persons.

realistic (apart from its meaning with reference to "realism" in literature and the arts) is a vogue-word (see 34), used instead of **practical**, with reference to "opinion", "view", "attitude", "plan", "action", as opposed to "theoretical", "ideal"; or, loosely, in the sense of **expedient, sensible, effective** or even **true** (as opposed to "unrealistic" for "false"). Its precise meaning in many contexts in which it appears is often not clear.

258   PRACTICALLY, VIRTUALLY, ALMOST, NEARLY

Careful speakers and writers restrict **practically** to the sense of "in practice", "in effect", with explicit or implicit contrast to something existing in theory. "However strange the idea may be it works out all right practically." "During the illness of Mr. Smith he was practically Managing Director." The word, however, is commonly used today as equivalent to **almost, nearly.** "He is practically a teetotaller." To **virtually** in this sense there is not the same objection as to **practically** with its other distinctive sense, but unaffected writing generally prefers the simplicity of **almost** or **nearly.**

The substitution of **almost** or **nearly** in negative statements would not be idiomatic: e.g. in "There was almost (or nearly) no water left". The idiom could be "any" qualified by "hardly", "scarcely", "barely".

PRAISE, EULOGY, EULOGIUM, ENCOMIUM 259

praise is the general word, and is applied to persons or things. **eulogy** is the word used for deliberately composed, studied **praise.** *C.O.D.* defines it as "praise in speech or writing of a person", but it can be applied directly to what is done, as well as to the doer: e.g. to a book, not less than to a writer. The Latin form, **eulogium,** sometimes used, is an affection of the sham-erudite (see 15). **encomium** (of Greek derivation) is another show-word, for high-flown **praise.**

PRECISENESS, PRECISION 260

preciseness is sometimes applied to action: e.g. with reference to religious observance, or strictness of behaviour ("The Puritan in his preciseness . . ."), but it is generally applied to careful accuracy in speech or writing. **precision** is restricted to action. Instructions, directions, explanations, definitions are expressed with **preciseness;** a measurement is taken with **precision.** We speak of "mathematical precision" and of "precision instruments".

The noun **prejudice** (by its Latin derivation="prejudging") primarily means "preconceived opinion". It is to be noted that this can be against or in favour of a person or thing. "I had no prejudice against him on this account." "I admit I have a strong prejudice in his favour." It is therefore a pity to use it, as is often done, in the sense of "harmful action", even though this use goes back two and a half centuries, when there exist the word **damage** and others: e.g. "injury", "harm", "disadvantage", "hurt", strong enough to do the job. This consideration applies also to a similar use of the verb **prejudice**, the adjective **prejudicial**, and the adverb **prejudicially**.

262 PREREQUISITE, PRECONDITION, CONDITION

prerequisite is a vogue-word (see 34) for a **condition** that has to be accepted or agreed to before discussion, negotiations, etc., can be entered into about some other matters at issue. "A truce in Palestine is the prerequisite of the proposed negotiation." "The British note to Russia has made it clear that the restoration of communications with Berlin is a prerequisite of a discussion on Germany as a whole." In neither sentence does this clumsy word convey any meaning that would not be provided by **condition** or **requisite**. **precondition** is an equally unnecessary word.

263   PRESUME, ASSUME

The two words are roughly synonymous in the sense of "take for granted", and so "suppose", "believe", "take it".

presume is used with reference to what the presumer believes, till it is disproved, to be true (*M.E.U.*). "Dr. Livingstone, I presume." "I presume she will accept the invitation'.

assume is used with reference to something the assumer takes for granted when on the strength of this belief he takes some step in thought or action. "I assume he has received my telegram, and I will now write to him to suggest an interview." "If we assume he left Moscow on Monday we can expect him to be home by now, and I will ring him up tomorrow."

presume has come to have the meaning also of "take improper advantage of." "He presumed on our slight acquaintance to ask me for a loan." The underlying idea here is that he (improperly, unjustifiably, without sufficient grounds) "took for granted that our slight acquaintance entitled him to ask me for such a favour".

PRESUMPTION, ASSUMPTION, HYPOTHESIS, 264
POSTULATE

presumption corresponds in sense to its verb **presume** (see last article), and means the acceptance of the truth of something till the contrary is proved. "The presumption must be that he never received the letter." An **assumption** and a **hypothesis** both mean a supposition made, without any reference to its truth, as a basis for reasoning (*C.O.D.*). **assumption** is the word that would generally be used with reference to a discussion or argument in the course of social intercourse, a debate, etc. **hypothesis** is generally used with reference to the starting-point in a serious inquiry.

postulate (by derivation, Latin, "something demanded") also means a supposition made as a basis for reasoning, but is generally used with reference to a philosophical argument rather than to a scientific or mathematical inquiry.

In geometry a **postulate** is a claim to take for granted the possibility of a "simple operation, e.g. of drawing a straight line between any two points" (*C.O.D.*).

In their synonymous uses **pretend** and **affect** imply that what a person or thing professes to be or to do is false, is feigned. On the other hand **purport** and **claim**, unless they are qualified by an adverb like "falsely", are used in a neutral sense without an implication of either truth or falsity. "He pretends he has read the book" implies that he has not read it; "She affected surprise" implies that she was not really surprised. "He purports to have read the book" leaves open the question whether he has done so. "It is claimed that the box contains all the documents originally entrusted to him" leaves open the question whether it does so.

For **claim** see also 317.

266   PRIDE, HAUGHTINESS, ARROGANCE, VANITY, CONCEIT

There can be what is called "proper" **pride**: e.g. in a clever son, in a friendship with a great man, in the prize you won at a horticultural show, in being independent of help. The other words always imply unpleasing qualities.

haughtiness generally implies a manner indicating a sense of one's superiority; **arrogance** an overbearing expression of one's demands or opinions; **vanity** and **conceit** excessive estimate of one's abilities or attractions.

In *Pride and Prejudice* Mary Bennett draws a distinction between **pride** and **vanity**: "Pride relates more to our opinion of ourselves, vanity to what we would have others think of us".

267   PRIMARY, PRIME, PREMIER, CHIEF, FIRST, PRIMAL

In their meaning of "highly important" these words are synonymous ("This is a matter of primary, prime, etc., consideration"), but *C.O.D.* enters **premier** as "now chiefly slang": e.g. in the description of a horse as gaining in a race "premier place". **primal** is rare.

For the relations of these words to each other in other senses see dictionary.

PROCEED, GO, COME 268

In military language **proceed** is a recognized word for **go**. Thus a unit is said to **proceed** to a depot. For ordinary purposes, however, **proceed** for **go** is journalese. If you have a fortnight's holiday and spend a part of it at Margate, you do not **proceed**, but you **go** there. If after a week you leave for another place, you may perhaps **proceed** there if you despise **go on** or **move**. The word should be restricted to the sense of something that "continues to be done". "She washed the socks and proceeded to darn them." "The judge overruled the objections and the case proceeded."

> And these have smaller fleas to bite 'em,
> And so proceed ad infinitum.   (Swift)

proceed is used also in journalese for **come, result, originate, arise,** or merely **happen.** "What lends an added interest to these documents is the fact that they proceeded from von Papen, the German ambassador in Ankara." "Serious confusion has proceeded from this ambiguous statement."

PRODUCT, PRODUCE 269

Both words mean the **result** of something, but, with referenec to concrete things, **product** is generally restricted to manufactured things, and **produce** to agricultural yield. **product,** but not **produce,** can be used figuratively: "This report was the product of many months' research"; and we speak of the "product of the imagination."

proffer and **tender** are show-words (see 15) for **offer** in its figurative use, with reference to help, advice, apology, resignation, etc.

271   PROPOSITION, PROPOSAL, PLAN

proposition means primarily and properly **statement, assertion**. "The proposition that Britain's economic recovery can be gained only by hard work, increased production, and restraint in demands for higher wages and an immediate higher standard of living, is an austere one that will not find ready support in many sections of the community." "The writer has confused the proposition that the Socialist Party cannot oppose Communism with the proposition that they are indistinguishable." Similarly we speak of a "self-evident proposition". The word, however, has come to be used for many meanings already amply provided for by existing words: especially **proposal, plan, scheme** (how tired we are of hearing about a "paying proposition"!) and also **job, problem, objective, prospect, suggestion, idea**, etc. *M.E.U.* delivers a two-column attack on the debased use of the word, which it says should be restored to its former well-defined functions, especially in logic and mathematics, and be relieved of its new status as "Jack-of-all-trades". When, however, we find a Professor of English Literature, in a book on English Composition, describing an invitation to deliver a certain course of lectures in certain circumstances as a "staggering proposition", there does not seem to be much hope of this.

272   PROTAGONIST, CHAMPION

By derivation **protagonist** (Greek *protagonistes*="first actor") means an actor on the stage taking the most important part in the drama; hence the one person who is most conspicuous in a struggle, cause, movement, story. In this strict sense there cannot be with reference to any given circumstances more than one **protagonist**. "There were many eminent and powerful supporters of the movement, but he was manifestly the protagonist." The *Oxford English Dictionary* recognizes, as a secondary meaning, that of "a leading personage in any contest, a prominent supporter or champion in any cause", and cites John Morley for so using it in 1877. In this sense the word is used as a synonym of **champion** both in the singular, where the **champion** is only one among others, and in the plural, with reference to two or more **champions**; similarly as a synonym of **defender, advocate, partisan, leader, supporter,** etc. Thus, with the indefinite article, a limiting adjective, etc., a person is described as "a protagonist", "a chief protagonist", "the chief protagonist", "the senior protagonist"; we are told that the author of a book wrote it "as a protagonist of Admiral Jellicoe"; and, with reference to an event, movement, etc., that "one (or two or many) of the protagonists are now dead". This extension of the word may have been due, Fowler suggests, to the erroneous idea that the first three letters, **pro-**, stood for the Latin preposition *pro* (=for, on behalf of), whereas it is the first four letters, **prot-**, that stand for the Greek adjective *protos* (=first). However that may be—and derivation cannot always be the court of appeal on the legitimate use of a word—this secondary use is to be deplored. Variety may be the spice of life, but there is no useful purpose, as is pointed out elsewhere, in cluttering up the language with an extension of a word's meaning when there already exist established words covering the senses in which the extension is used. Moreover this use of **protagonist** tends to obliterate the original and distinctive sense, in which the word has useful work to do. (Compare **anticipate** (7), **aggravating** (169).

It does not follow from the examples given above of the use of **protagonists**, with reference to a single event, movement, etc., that the word cannot ever be used in the plural with strict propriety in its primary meaning. It can be if it refers, not to more than one person in a given event, movement, etc., but to a total number made up by one person each in a number of events, movements, etc. "The protagonists in these three plays [i.e. one in each] remind us of characters of Ibsen's." "In the Spanish Civil War the two initial protagonists [i.e. one on each side] were Franco and Caballero."

273   PRUDENT, PRUDENTIAL

prudential is generally restricted to being descriptive of the motive, considerations, etc., actuating conduct, and is not applied either to conduct itself or to a person. **prudent** refers to conduct or to a person. A general is **prudent**; he takes a **prudent** course; he is influenced, and his course is marked, by **prudential** considerations.

274   PSYCHOLOGICAL, SUITABLE

In the vogue-phrase **psychological moment** the adjective is given the meanings of **suitable, opportune, critical, one and only,** with reference to a state of suspense, crisis, danger, etc. The phrase seems to have originated in a German one, in which **moment** stood, not for a unit of time, but for **momentum.** However that may be, the English phrase, with the philosophical associations of the adjective, have been taken up eagerly by journalists anxious to impress their readers. Its application is often absurdly inept. Thus in the gardening notes of a newspaper we are told that "the present showery weather provides a psychological moment for transplanting lettuce seedlings".

275   PUPIL, STUDENT, SCHOLAR, TRAINEE

In their roughly synonymous senses a **pupil** is a learner up to the end of school age (usually at a school); a **student** is a learner beyond school age (usually at a university or other place of advanced instruction). There are, however, special uses of both words. Thus an architect is said to have **pupils**, who would be beyond school age; and **student** can apply to a person of any age who devotes himself to a branch of learning. **scholar** still survives, especially among teachers in primary schools, for any child attending school; otherwise the word used is **pupil**, and **scholar** is restricted to the winner of a scholarship at a school or a university, or to a person versed in literature. **trainee** is one of the latest inventions of nouns ending in **ee** for a person undergoing training in preparation for special work, especially of a technical sort. It is beginning to be used also as an adjective: e.g. "trainee engineer" (on the analogy of "student teacher").

PUPPET, MARIONETTE 276

Strictly **puppet** is the general word and **marionette** is a particular sort of **puppet**. A **puppet** is any small figure used for dramatic purposes. Controlled by strings it is called a **marionette**. In ordinary speech and writing, and even in dictionaries, these two words are treated as synoynms. **puppet**, however, is the word generally applied metaphorically to human beings, though W. S. Gilbert in *The Mikado* used **marionette**: "Do you think we are worked with strings like a commonplace marionette?" **puppet** in its metaphorical use often refers contemptuously to one who serves servilely to further another's aims, but Browning, in *Pippa Passes*, has

> God's puppets, best and worst,
Are we.

(For help over this article I am indebted to Mrs. Nancy Henry, of "The Henry Puppets".)

277   PURCHASE, BUY

As a verb **purchase** is a genteelism (see 85) for **buy**.

As a noun, however, **purchase** is an ordinary working word, for there is not a noun of the same stem corresponding to **buy** except in slang: "That was a good buy" (="a good purchase", "a good bargain").

278   QUIESCENT, QUIET

quiescent implies, as **quiet** need not, that a condition of inactivity etc. is only a temporary one.

279   QUOTE, CITE

In most contexts the words could be interchanged. When any distinction is recognizable **quote** implies the repetition of words, spoken or written, whereas **cite** implies a reference in general terms.

quote is sometimes used as an unnecessary substitute for **mention**. "He quoted several occasions when her conduct had been suspicious." "Some of the instances I have quoted . . ."

quote is also a commercial term for stating the price of something (a commodity to be sold, work to be done, etc.), as is also its noun **quotation**.

cite has also a legal meaning=to summon to appear in court.

280   REACTION, RESPONSE

response means **reply, answer**, literally in words, figuratively in action, to words or action. **reaction** in its primary sense means in physiology organic response to stimulus. Thence it has come to be used for action taken as a counterstroke, especially at first in a military sense. In an extension of this meaning it has become established in recent years as synonymous for **response, answer**, as shown in the feelings, opinions, criticism, etc., evoked by something done, said, written. "The Council has expressed its reaction to the announcement." "Please study this scheme and let me know your reactions" (which means nothing more than "tell me what you think"). The word is badly overworked.

READY, PREPARED, WILLING 281

ready and **prepared** (followed by "to") in the sense of **willing** (to), or equivalent merely to **will** or **would**, are circumlocutions, especially in officialese and commercialese. "We are ready to accept your offer . . ." "We will be prepared to consider your application if you will fill up the enclosed form." "I am prepared to admit . . ."

REALIZE, KNOW 282

realize has for its primary meaning "make real", "turn into fact." "At last his ambition was realized." "My worst fears were realized." With a second and extremely common meaning today it is used instead of **know** when the speaker or writer wishes to emphasize not merely that he is aware of the matter referred to, but that he has a keen, vivid consciousness of it with a full understanding of all the cirstances and implications. "I did not complain of the delay because I realized all the difficulties he had had to contend with". "I realize that what you have said expresses only your view and does not commit your co-directors."

REALLY, ACTUALLY, POSITIVELY, 283
ABSOLUTELY, LITERALLY, VERITABLY

In their roughly synonymous relation these six adverbs are generally mere emphasizers: "the familiar herald of a strained top note". Sometimes more effect would be gained if the word or phrase they qualify were left bare without any adornment. At other times the use of one of these adverbs is the resource of a speaker or writer failing from laziness to choose a more precise word or phrase that could dispense with an emphasizer.

The worst offender is **literally**. There are few sentences in which the word adds anything to the meaning. It is sometimes used to qualify a word that already is emphatic: e.g. "He was literally exhausted". As exhaustion itself is an extreme stage, **literally** does not add to the sense. "Amateur gardeners can now ensure themselves a supply of duty-free tobacco literally at a cost of 1d. or 2d. an ounce." What faintest shade of difference is made here by the inclusion of the word **literally** to the bare statement without it? "In Bournemouth I came to know literally thousands of people." That one's acquaintances at a single town should number thousands is itself a remarkable experience. How is the strength of the statement increased by **literally**? Cannot the reader be left to assume that the writer means what he says and is truthful and accurate? Worse than mere pleonasm of this sort is the absurdity when the writer, while implicitly professing to be using "literal" language, uses a metaphor. Consider one of the examples of this misuse given in *M.E.U.*: "H. B. Stallard in the half-mile literally flew round the track". This sentence was recently shown to a youngster of fifteen, who, though he knew more about aeroplanes than literary style, after a moment's scrutiny answered: "As it was a running race, surely he would have been disqualified". One recent letter to *The Times* quoted a statement that "for five years Mr. Gladstone was literally glued to the Treasury Bench". Another letter to the same paper lamented a deterioration in the game of rackets through recourse to dynamite when one reads that a player "literally blasted his opponent out of court".

When **veritably** is not merely an emphasizer, as an imagined improvement on **really, actually, positively, absolutely,** its function, like that of its adjective **veritable**—says Fowler sarcastically—is, if one contemplates an exaggeration, to say compendiously, but seldom truthfully, "I am not exaggerating". "Veritably a stream of curses issued from his lips."

recondition is a recently introduced word. Its detractors can argue that, if it is to be regarded as formed from the verb "to condition", the sense in which it is used has no relation to any of the established meanings of that verb; or alternatively that, if it is regarded as formed from the noun "condition", to which in sense it does have a relation, the prefix of **re** to a noun in order to make a verb is unusual and clumsy. Nevertheless in its meaning of "overhaul, thoroughly repair, and make as new", it is convenient for implying more than does any of its nearest synonyms: **renovate, repair, refit, reconstruct.** Take for example an Atlantic liner requisitioned by the Admiralty in the last war, converted into a troopship, and after the war restored to its original condition. To **recondition** this ship is more than to **repair** it or **renovate** it; to **refit** suggests still less: rather redecoration and refurnishing; to **reconstruct** implies restriction to structural alteration; even to **reconvert** sounds somewhat too general: whereas **reconditioning** conveys the idea of a process of detailed alterations.

There is a tendency of the English language to acquire new words that, though they may at first appear unnecessary, yet gradually become used in a specialized sense. **renovate** may come to be used for one kind of mending and making new, **recondition** for another. Thus we shall perhaps **renovate** but not **recondition** our clothes, and **recondition** but not **renovate** our engines and mechanical gadgets.

RECRIMINATIONS, ACCUSATIONS, CHARGES   285

recrimination in the plural is often used when the proper word would be **accusations** or **charges.** The cause of its popularity is no doubt that to lovers of long words its five syllables seem to give it extra force. It should be restricted to **accusations** that are counter or mutual.

Some years ago **redundant** was generally used with reference to excess or repetition in speaking or writing. The word is now common with reference to employees in industry, business, etc., who are **superfluous, unnecessary**, because there is no longer enough work to need their continued employment. In a slovenly construction it is used to qualify, not the employees, but the factory, office, etc., where they work: which should mean that the whole factory, office, etc., is **superfluous**.

287 REFER, ALLUDE, ADVERT

To **refer** is to draw attention to a thing or person directly. Thus in the present book the Oxford dictionaries are often **referred** to. To **allude** is to draw attention indirectly: "No doubt the writer is here alluding to Shaw's early books"; or covertly "Are you alluding to me?" (sc. "It looks as if you are"). **advert** is officialese. "Adverting to your letter of June 23rd I am to tell you . . ."

288 REGARDING, RESPECTING, CONCERNING, ANENT, RE

regarding, respecting, relating, concerning, and a number of corresponding phrases "as regards", "in relation to", etc., are officialese for **about** or **on**. "We hope to write to you again shortly regarding this matter." "It is difficult to form a closer opinion respecting future prospects in the industry." A good writer will avoid these until a better case can be made for them than that they are often used.

anent is archaic, and like a number of other archaisms is sometimes an affectation of journalese.

re (Latin="in the matter of") is legal or commercial jargon. Used in ordinary speaking or writing for **about** it is a vulgarism.

For the established meanings of the verb **register** see dictionary. These include the **recording** in writing of a fact, name, entry, etc.; and, with reference to a measuring instrument, **recording** automatically. In journalese the word is used, in the sense of **show**, with reference to a person's voice, facial impression, manner: "His face registered surprise". This use had probably come from Hollywood where actors and actresses, when being photographed, are told to "register" the emotion considered suitable to the situation. In further unnecessary extensions the word is made to serve for a number of words and phrases: "realize", "feel", "notice", "be conscious of", "store up in memory", etc., used so loosely that the precise meaning in a given context is often obscure.

REGRET, BE SORRY, DEPLORE, LAMENT   290

be sorry, followed by "for", "about", or a noun clause ("He was sorry about this"; "I am sorry he did it"), is the working phrase, but **regret**, though it is also used suitably for formal purposes, is nearly as common as **be sorry**, perhaps partly on account of its one word instead of two, and partly because **sorry** is so much used in absolute constructions: "I can only say I am sorry"; "Sorry!"

deplore and **lament** express a high degree of sorrow or disapproval.

REHABILITATION, RESTORATION   291

rehabilitation and the verb **rehabilitate** are in frequent use today with reference to the multitude of post-war economic, social and political problems. They are not new words, though originally they were restricted to the restoration of a degraded man's rank and privileges; then, up to the last war, they were used chiefly with reference to the re-establishment of a person's reputation.

Sir Alan Herbert condemns **rehabilitation** as ugly and

unnecessary, and says **restoration** covers all the meanings needed. Certainly both the noun and its verb are sometimes used when simpler words could serve the purposes: e.g. "We are devoting too little of our resources to rehabilitating the volume of exports". Mr. Ivor Brown in *Just Another Word* agrees with Sir Alan Herbert in disliking the words, which he describes as the darlings of Government departments. In particular he deprecates their application by the Ministry of Health to the treatment of diseased and wounded people, and sarcastically wonders whether the next translation of the Bible will speak, not of healing the sick, but of **rehabilitating** those suffering from psychophysical maladjustment. Sir Ernest Gowers in *Plain Words*, while deploring their official use for "everything from houses to invalids", points out that **rehabilitation** in its use by the Ministry of Health means something more than healing: namely a course of treatment or instruction for the purpose of restoring people already healed of diseases or wounds to a life of active usefulness. As this extension of the healing art, he adds, was a new conception, it was reasonably given a new name, however ill-chosen that name may be.

The words therefore cannot be dismissed as merely voguewords (see 34). Even in a more general reference than that cited by Sir Ernest Gowers their modern use supplies a sense for new conditions resulting from the last war that no other single words do. "The offer of the loan to Malaya for financing compensation for war damage is conditional on the British Government's being satisfied that the scheme for this is an effective instrument of rehabilitation." The words have become established both in general and in official use. Thus there is now a "British Council for Rehabilitation", and New Zealand has a "Minister of Rehabilitation".

292 REMARK, COMMENT, OBSERVATION

In some contexts the three words would be interchangeable. When a distinction is recognizable a **remark** is more commonly used for a short, casual spoken utterance: "As we walked along my companion made the remark that he had never seen so few grouse on this moor". A **comment** or **observation** is more commonly used for a considered and set-out statement, spoken or written, and often critical, with reference to something that has been spoken or written, or that has happened. "My comment at this stage is that the proposal represents only a long-term policy, but what is needed is an immediate palliative." "Has the witness any observation to make about the accident?" In official circles a civil servant receiving a memorandum or minute is often asked to give his "obs." (**observations**): not his **comments**.

REMEMBER, RECOLLECT, RECALL, 293
REMINISCE

remember generally implies an effortless process of the mind; **recollect** and **recall**, a mental process with conscious effort, deliberately collecting, bringing together, gathering up, the fragments of past actions, events, thoughts, feelings. Wordsworth defined poetry as taking its origin "from emotion recollected in tranquillity".

reminisce corresponds in meaning to **reminiscence** (see 200), but unlike the noun is generally used only colloquially.

The adjective **reminiscent**, besides its meaning corresponding to that of **reminiscence** and **reminisce**, can mean reminding or suggesting. "Some of his poetry is reminiscent of A. E. Housman's *Shropshire Lad*."

REMITTANCE, MONEY 294

remittance (Latin *remittere*="to send back") is used as a commercial term for **money** in any form sent by post. In business it is a conveniently comprehensive word for covering, without the need of specification, cheques, postal orders, or what not, with reference to money that has to be sent or that has been received, especially for use in a printed form: e.g. "We acknowledge the receipt of your remittance for . . ." "I enclose a remittance for . . ." "A remittance should accompany your order". Used, however, in privately personal relations it is a genteelism (see 85).

The verb **remit** for send is a genteelism in private speech or correspondence; otherwise it is commercialese or officialese.

A "remittance man" (now almost obsolete) is a man living abroad whose source of income is derived from **money** sent him regularly by someone at home.

295   REMOVE, TAKE AWAY

remove has a long and honourable history.

> God is in the midst of her, therefore shall she not
>   be removed.   (Book of Common Prayer)

Nevertheless today in ordinary speaking and writing it would strike a pompous note (see 15), and most of us would follow Oliver Cromwell, who did not say "Remove these baubles".

296   RENDER, MAKE

render has a long and honourable history. It is frequently found in the Authorized Version of the Bible. Shakespeare used it in various senses. In current idiom it has a number of uses. As a synonym, however, for **make** in the sense of "cause to be" it is a show-word (see 15). "Illness rendered it impossible for him to attend the ceremony." From a gardening paper: "This will render the plants more robust".

See also next article.

For **render**="cause to be" see last article. In another sense also the verb is a show-word, used by announcers of musical programmes and by music critics for **singing** a song and **playing** an instrumental piece of music.

Worse still, they speak and write of such **rendering** as a **rendition**. (Properly **rendition**, now rare, means "surrender" of a place or person.)

REPAST, COLLATION, MEAL 298

repast, for a rich meal, and **collation** for a light one (and not at the usual time for a meal), are archaic and journalese. **collation** is said to derive its name from the practice of reading the *Collations* (Lives of the Fathers of the Church) during meals in monasteries.

REPEAT, REITERATE, ITERATE 299

All three words are given in *C.O.D.* as meaning doing something, or stating something in speech or writing, a second time, but **reiterate** and (rare) **iterate** are today restricted to statement.

RESIDE, DWELL, LIVE 300

reside, as a substitute for **live**, with reference to the place where a person has his permanent home, is what Sir Alan Herbert might call a snob-word: see example in next article. **dwell** is journalese for **live**.

RESIDENCE, MANSION, ABODE, DOMICILE, 301 DWELLING, HOUSE, HOME

house is the working word.

mansion by etymology (Latin *manere*="to remain") means "abiding-place."

> Can storied urn or animated bust
> Back to its mansion call the fleeting breath?
>
> (Gray's *Elegy*)

The Mansion House is the official "abiding-place" of the Lord Mayor of London. Then the word was applied to any large house for living in. "Mansions" is often used in the name of a building divided into residential flats. Otherwise today **mansion** is not used except as auctioneers' and house agents' trade jargon ("This imposing Georgian mansion"), or as a snob-word: the Mrs. Jones who **donates** (see 127) £5 to a hospital, and **disposes of** (see 322) a fur coat she **purchased** (see 277) many years ago, left London during the war to **reside** (see last article) in her country **mansion**.

residence also is today auctioneers' and house agents' jargon: "This desirable residence". **abode** is archaic. So is **domicile** except in a legal sense for **home**, "permanent place of living". **dwelling**, a word not much used now, is a **house** of a humble kind.

302   RESORT, RECOURSE, RESOURCE

In their meaning the words are closely synonymous, but distinctions are shown in the main idiomatic phrases in which they are used. Treble and Vallins in *An ABC of English Usage* tabulate these as follows:

recourse: "to have recourse or resort"; "without recourse or resort".

resort: "in the last resort".

resource: "as a last resource"; "the only resource"; "at the end of his resources".

303   RESULT, CONSEQUENCE, EFFECT,
AFTERMATH, REPERCUSSION

In some contexts **result, consequence, effect** could be interchanged. "A **result** (or **consequence** or **effect**) of this mistake of his was that he was dismissed from his post." In other contexts a distinction between **result** and **consequence** is discernible. **result** may refer to something following so closely some given action, etc., that it is thought of as a part, a final stage, of it: e.g. with reference to a horse race, athletic contest, examination, we talk of a **result**, not a **consequence**. Even when the sequence in time is not so close as this, **result** is commonly used for an occurrence that marks the end of an action or a series of actions, whereas **consequence** is more commonly used for what follows remotely or indirectly. Thus we would probably say that the (immediate) **result** of the last war was the defeat of Germany, but it would be slightly more idiomatic to describe the present shortage of goods in the world as a **consequence** than a **result** of the war. A cause of preference for **consequence** to **result** may be that the length of the word gives it an onomatopoeic effect for conditions, etc., long drawn out. Compare **difficult** (71) and **endeavour** (89).

Where distinctions are recognizable **effect** would range with **result** rather than with **consequence** in its use with reference to an immediate sequence of events. Thus we should probably speak of the **effects** or **results** of an explosion rather than its **consequences**. **effect**, however, is used less commonly than the two other words.

aftermath (Old English *math*="mowing") means primarily "late or second sowing", or "the crop of grass sprung up after the mowing in early summer". For the earliest figurative use of the word the *Oxford English Dictionary* cites some lines in a poem of the middle of the seventeenth century (ascribed, probably wrongly, to John Cleveland), with reference to a young man who has as mistress an old widow.

> Rash Lover speak what pleasure hath
> Thy Spring in such an Aftermath?

It has now become a vogue-word (see 34), used sometimes also in the plural, for **result, consequence, effect**. Mr.

Winston Churchill uses it as the sub-title of one of the volumes of *The World Crisis*, and it has appeared as the title of a recent book of poems. It is frequently applied to the economic and social **consequences** of the last war, and, though the primary meaning of the word implies a crop that is of some value, nearly always to conditions that are undesirable. This usage might be defended as providing in one word what otherwise would need more than one: e.g. "bad consequences", but it is a pity that a pretty word remindful of "Flora and the country green" and of beneficial harvest should be applied to associations so grimly alien.

repercussion literally means the recoil of a thing after impact. In a figurative extension it has become a vogue-word for **result, consequence, effect**, usually of one that is indirect or remote or unintended. In this sense it can perhaps serve a purpose. "The immediate result of the release of the atomic bomb was the surrender of Japan. Its repercussions were to determine American foreign policy and decisively end isolationism by showing that neither Monroe doctrine nor oceans could henceforth protect American homes from destruction." When, however, it is used without any such implications, as a substitute for **result**, etc., it is merely a long and high-sounding show-word of the sham erudite (see 15). "These events in Moscow will have repercussions all over the world."

304   RESULT, ACCRUE

accrue is legal jargon used in financial statements, wills, etc., with reference to interest on invested money or other monetary advantage. "It was pointed out that against the cost of redecorating and furnishing might be set any rent accruing from the letting of the rooms." It has no advantage over the simple words **result, come**, and it is generally pleonastic as in the sentence quoted, where it adds no sense sense to "rent from". It has been seized by users of show-words as a substitute, without any financial implication, for **result, come, happen.** "The benefits accruing to the average allotment holder are insufficient to justify so extensive a curtailment of amenities." "Nobody can say what would have happened if no foreign help had accrued to the other side." Sometimes it is used in an absolute construction: "Several unfortunate complications have accrued".

RESUME, CONTINUE 305

An action that has been begun can be gone on with (*a*) continuously, (*b*) after a break. **continue** can apply to either condition. (*a*) "He was so much interested in the book that he continued reading it into the small hours." (*b*) "When these interruptions subsided he continued his speech." **resume** is a show-word (see 15) for **continue** in sense (*b*), to which it is restricted. "After the lunch interval Bradman resumed his innings."

RETALIATION, REPRISAL 306

Both words mean "repayment of injury in kind". **reprisal** is generally used for such an act of repayment in war; **retaliation** in other circumstances.

RETICENT, SECRETIVE, TACITURN 307

reticent and **secretive** can refer (*a*) to a person's behaviour in a particular situation, or (*b*) to his habitual behaviour. **taciturn** refers only to (*b*).

reticent=disinclined to say what one knows and feels.

taciturn=addicted to few words; habitually silent: i.e. **reticent** in a manner that is ungenial.

secretive=extremely **reticent.**

RETREAT, RETIRE, WITHDRAW 308

retreat is generally used with reference to military operations. **retire** also is used in a similar military sense, but more commonly it is applied figuratively to a person who permanently leaves his employment or other occupation. The genteel **retire** to bed. **withdraw** (intransitively) is a formal word for formal occasions (e.g. after a ceremonial visit).

309   RETRIEVE, FIND, RECOVER, REGAIN,
            GET BACK

retrieve (French *retrouver*="to find again") was used primarily, as it still is, with reference to dogs finding game (compare the noun "retriever"). Thence it came to mean in a general application **recover, regain, get back**. In a figurative sense it is used idiomatically with reference to fortune, honour, etc. "It is hoped that this action by the United States will retrieve the military situation in South Korea." As a synonym merely for **recover**, etc., with reference to a concrete object it is a show-word (see 15). "Police-constable Cashley retrieved the dog that had fallen down the shaft." Why **retrieved** instead of **found** or **rescued**? "The last three letters of his I was able to retrieve from my files had been written at Davos." Why not **find** in or **recover** from? It is sometimes used with the mere sense of **get, obtain, procure**, without reference to anything that has been lost. "For the door of the shed I was able to retrieve some timber that had been dumped on the common."

310   REVEAL, DISPLAY, MANIFEST, EXHIBIT,
            DISCLOSE, EVINCE, SHOW

As substitutes for **show** in the sense of "give signs of" all these verbs are show-words (see 15). "The author reveals a subtle sense of humour." "He displayed (or manifested, exhibited, disclosed, evinced) great alarm at the news." The use of **reveal** in this way is especially undesirable, for the word (by derivation="unveil") has a distinct meaning of "bring to light", literally or figuratively, something that before was hidden or unknown. "Drawing aside a panel he revealed a cupboard stored with explosives." "The plot now stood revealed." "He would not reveal what decisions had been reached."

rich and **wealthy** are as closely synonymous as words can be. When the longer word **wealthy** is used, the explanation is probably that the speaker or writer is influenced unconsciously by the fact that **rich** has many other meanings besides the primary one: e.g. there is a **rich** cake, a **rich** colour, a **rich** joke. *C.O.D.* has seventeen lines for **rich** and only six for **wealthy**. Compare **alter** (29), **difficult** (71), **endeavour** (89), **expensive** (101).

rich and **wealthy** can refer to an individual or to a firm, company, family, society, country. The use of **opulent** and **affluent** is restricted to an individual. **opulent** generally implies outward signs of being **rich**. **affluent** has today a somewhat archaic air.

The common corresponding noun to **rich** is the plural word **riches**. **richness** is rare, and is generally used only figuratively: e.g. of a writer's vocabulary. **wealth** is often used in a general sense with reference to the basic or other resources of a country.

RIDE, DRIVE   312

(1) One **rides** (*a*) in a vehicle that is controlled by another: e.g. omnibus, train; or (*b*) on an animal: e.g. horse, camel.

(2) One **drives**, or is **driven**, (*a*) in a vehicle controlled by oneself: e.g. pony-cart, motor-car, for even if one has a coachman or a chauffeur one indirectly controls the vehicle; (*b*) in a vehicle hired, and so indirectly controlled, by oneself: e.g. taxicab.

An inconsistency seems to be involved in **riding** (not **driving**) a bicycle, which one controls. Here, however, one is on a saddle, and the idea of control implicit in the word **riding**, as on the saddle of a horse—see 1 (*b*)—has been extended to the progress on both a push-bicycle and a motor-cycle.

313   ROOM, ROOMS, ACCOMMODATION, APARTMENT, LODGING

These words are synonymous in the sense of temporary living quarters. A **room, rooms,** and **accommodation** may refer to furnished or unfurnished places; **apartment** and (generally in the plural, and, even so, seldom used today) **lodging** are restricted to furnished places. **accommodation** is a more general word for room-space that is supplied, especially with food at an inn.

In law **lodgers** are people living in a house whose owner himself lives in it or manages it by himself. Otherwise they are **tenants**.

314   SABOTAGE, DAMAGE

The verb **sabotage** and its nouns were not many years ago used only with reference to the **damage** done to plant by disaffected workmen. Today, as a vogue-word (see 34), they are used in a general sense with reference to the deliberate doing of **damage**, material or figurative: **wrecking, injuring, spoiling**, etc. "Marshal Sokolovsky's statement accused the British and Americans of seeking to sabotage the preparation of the report." "The official statement calls the action of the eastern zone an attempt to sabotage the conference."

The noun **saboteur** is used in the same way.

315   SAME, IT, THIS, THEM, THESE

same is used in commercial jargon for **it, this, them, these.** "We have received your order for a lawn-mower, and shall deliver same as soon as it comes from the factory."

316   SAVE, EXCEPT, BUT

save, which as a preposition meaning **except, but**, has a long and honourable tradition in poetic and oratorical use ("They lost all save honour"), is today in ordinary speech and writing an archaism.

To **say** is the most general word to mean "express in speech or writing".

The use of **state** instead of **say** would be in many contexts formal (see 15), but there are occasions when what is expressed is itself of a formal character: e.g. in an announcement by a Minister in Parliament, or by an official publication. **state** is needed also where other words, including **say**, cannot be used, governing an object and not introducing a noun clause: "He stated his conditions briefly but firmly".

To **assert, affirm, declare, aver** are to **say** with emphasis. **aver**, apart from its use in law, has an archaic air.

To **announce** is to make known to a wide circle.

To **proclaim** is to **say** publicly, formally.

To **intimate** is used for making something known, giving information, in a less direct way than is generally done by **say**: for hinting rather than expressing explicitly and positively, often equivalent to **imply, suggest, give to understand.**

To **indicate** in its primary sense means to **show, point out,** literally and figuratively. "The height of the mercury in a thermometer indicates the temperature." "The smallness of the number of men Caesar lost in his campaigns indicates his greatness as a commander." (Here **indicates** means the same as **denotes.**) As a synonym of **say, state,** etc., it has the same sense of implying as has **intimate.** "I hoped the final sentence of my answer would indicate that I intend to give practical recognition of my views on the point." "Reports indicate that the railway line from the Russian zone to the west is now repaired and in order." In a colloquial extension, not recognized by *C.O.D.*, **indicate** is used to mean "suggest as desirable." "After several hours of steep ascent a short rest was now indicated before pressing on to the final pitch." This use is somewhat similar to a medical one, with reference to symptoms that **indicate, betoken, act as a sign for,** a certain treatment.

To **maintain,** in its relation to the other words treated here, means, like **assert, affirm, declare, aver,** to say with emphasis, but it often implies consciousness by the speaker that others may not admit the truth of what is said.

To **claim** is to **maintain,** but with the further implication that recognition is demanded of the truth of what is said. When used merely for **say** without these implications it is a vulgarism. See also 265.

allege is used, rather than **say,** with reference to something about which it is desired to emphasize that the truth is not, and in some circumstances may never be, known. Counsel for the prosecution: "The prisoner alleges that he was not in the house on that day". "In *Contemporary Portraits* Frank Harris alleged that Carlyle had confided to him some private facts about his married life." The word is often used in newspaper reports, in order that, by a guarded statement that something is only **alleged** to have been done or said, the danger of being sued for libel may be avoided.

318   SCOTCH, SCOTTISH, SCOT, SCOTS

Scotch and **Scots** are used both as adjectives and nouns; **Scot** properly only as a noun, though sometimes in a colloquial vulgarism as an adjective.

Scotch dates from the end of the sixteenth century. From England it travelled over the Border, and was adopted in Scotland before the end of the eighteenth century. It was used by Burns and later by Scott. Robert Louis Stevenson (1850–1894), born and bred in Scotland, and usually a punctilious writer, used indifferently **Scotch** and **Scottish.** Early in the present century, however, **Scotch** had fallen into disfavour, and gradually made way for the older form **Scottish.** Thus the "Scotch Education Department" became the "Scottish Education Department". Today an educated native of Scotland would describe himself as "Scottish", not "Scotch", and would not, for example, speak of "the Scotch" or "Scotch youth", "Scotch scenery", "the Scotch Highlands". He would reserve **Scotch** as an adjective for certain things specially associated with, originating from, in common use in, Scotland: e.g. "Scotch whisky", "Scotch broth", "Scotch tweeds".

Scot (noun) is a native of Scotland; plural **Scots**, i.e. an alternative for (the) "Scottish". In history books we read of "the Picts and the Scots".

Scots as a singular noun is the dialect of Scotland. It is also an adjective: e.g. "Scots Law"; the leading Edinburgh daily paper, *The Scotsman*; the regiment "the Scots Greys"; the celebrated train from King's Cross Station in London to Waverley Station in Edinburgh, "the Flying Scotsman"; similarly a "Scotsman", a "Scotswoman". In England, however, a native of Scotland is called a "Scotchman" or a "Scotchwoman".

SECTION, CROSS-SECTION, SAMPLE 319

section used figuratively is defined by *C.O.D.* as "part of a community having separate interests or characteristics". Thus the Conservative Party is a **section** of the community, consisting of persons who in their political opinions are identical, whether they are young or old, rich or poor, male or female, etc. **cross-section** (not yet admitted to *C.O.D.*), which is primarily a technical term used in engineering with reference to a drawing, is also now used figuratively for a part of the community, but with reference to a given population it is a group taken independently of any selective divisions: i.e. a collection of persons who are representative—that is the key-point of distinction—of different types, in the relative proportion to that in which it may be assumed they would be found in the whole population. The Conservative Party is not a **cross-section** of the community.

sample by itself without qualification by the adjective "representative" is hardly adequate to express fully the implication of **cross-section**. Thus in an announcement of the results of a Gallup Poll the question put is described correctly as having been answered by a "representative **sample** (i.e. **cross-section**) of men and women in England, Scotland and Wales". Journalese with its hankering for long and high-sounding synonyms of simple words often uses cross-section when all that is meant is **sample, specimen, example**.

320 SEE, PERCEIVE, DISCERN, DESCRY, ESPY

see is the common working word, physically with reference to the sight of concrete objects, figuratively with reference to apprehension by the mind. **perceive** and **discern** have the implication not merely that something comes before the eyes or is recognizable by the mind, but that this happens as a result of close scrutiny, inspection, examination, reflection. Used merely as a synonym of **see** without this implication they are show-words (see 15). **descry** and **espy** are comparatively rare, and are used only in a literal sense.

321 SEEK, SEARCH

seek, familiar to us in the language of the Bible ("Seek and ye shall find"; "Seek ye first the Kingdom of Heaven"), strikes today, as a synonym of **search** (for) and other senses (see dictionary), a somewhat archaic note. "We sought him at home, his office, his club, but nowhere was he to be found." "He sought in vain for a way out of the difficulty." "She decided to seek her brother's advice." It is idiomatic, but a cliché, in "The causes (or reasons) are far to seek"; and the passive compounds **sought for, sought after**, are not uncommon. For **seek**=**try** see 89.

dispose (of) is a genteelism (see 85). A shop frankly **sells** you its goods. Mrs. Jones's soul is above a commercial transaction, but she is willing to **dispose** of a fur coat for a good price.

SENSE, FEEL   323

The verb **sense** goes back to the seventeenth century, with the meaning of **perceive** (an outward object of the senses). At a much later date it came to be used for **feel** with the meaning of become aware more or less vaguely or instinctively. "Directly he entered the room he sensed a hostile attitude in the company." This use is disliked by some. Probably, however, it will become established, and with advantage to the language provided that journalese does not cause it to encroach on the use of **feel** in more general meanings. Nor is there any point in adopting an American use of it as a synonym of **understand, comprehend, know, realize, and even foresee.**

SENSUAL, SENSUOUS   324

sensual pertains to bodily pleasures, especially those of food and sex. A person is **sensual** if he is addicted to such sensual pleasures. **sensuous** pertains to thoughts and ideas derived from the senses. A person is **sensuous** if he is strongly moved in his imagination by beautiful sights and sounds and by objects that are pleasant to smell, taste and touch. A style of writing is **sensuous** if it draws many of its images from objects that affect the senses. Spenser's and Keats's poetry are notably **sensuous** (but not **sensual**). Milton, who apparently invented the word **sensuous**, said that poetry should be "simple, sensuous and passionate".

To **service** is a verb that is coming into use as a trade term for keeping in perfect order a customer's mechanical apparatus: motor-car, typewriter, etc. **maintain** is an established word that comes nearest to covering this idea, but an owner of a motor-car can be said in formal language to **maintain** it in the sense merely of possessing and using it. **service**, therefore, for "maintain in order", will probably establish itself. Compare **recondition** (284).

326   SERVIETTE, NAPKIN

serviette (a French word) is a genteelism for (table) **napkin**. **napkin** was formerly the word used for the square piece of linen for wiping the lips, fingers, etc., with at meals. Hotels and restaurants, always biased in favour of French words (e.g. in the names of dishes on the menu— itself a French word), introduced the word **serviette**. Genteel folk took this up, perhaps thinking it was a "nicer" word than one associative of hygienic towels. The drapers' shops followed suit, and today if a woman wishes to buy some table **napkins** the shopwalker and the assistants will firmly refuse to use any word for the articles they show madam except **serviette**.

327   SHADOW, SHADE

shadow is the patch of comparative darkness projected by a stationary or moving object that intercepts rays of light: e.g. a person can throw a **shadow** as he walks in strong sunlight; a tree can throw a **shadow** on a lawn. A **shadow** keeps something of the shape of the object throwing it. A **shade** is the resulting state of comparative darkness and often coolness. "Primroses do best when grown in shade."

The words have distinctive figurative uses. "This experience threw a lasting shadow on his life." "He was put in the shade by his younger brother."

"One of the most elaborate and wonderful achievements of the genius of the language," says Pearsall Smith, "is the differentiation of the uses of **shall** and **will**, a distinction not observed by earlier writers." The difficulty connected with the words is that the use for the first person ("I", "we") differs from that for the second and third persons. In the first person **will** and **would** are used when there is an idea of wishing, willing, desiring, intending; **shall** and **should** when the idea is merely of futurity. The following sentences illustrate the practice. "We shall never see his like again." "I will never yield on that point." "I shall be getting a whole month's holiday." "If I chose the Highlands I should see the heather in full bloom." "I would spend all my days in walking and fishing." "If we have hard times ahead—I will never admit the word 'despair' on British lips—we shall come through our difficulties in the end" (Mr. Winston Churchill, at Ayr, May 16th, 1947).

Even those who ordinarily preserve the distinction often ignore it when the verb to which the auxiliary is attached itself implies wishing; and one hears or reads e.g. "I would like to go"; "I would be grateful for suggestions". As "like" and "care" imply wishing, **would** here involves pleonasm. It implies also a psychological absurdity. Thus, whatever may be one's views of the nature of the will— whether it is free or determined—"to will to like or to care" is impossible. The tendency to use **would** instead of **should** may be due partly to the fact that **should** has, besides the sense of futurity, that of obligation. All of this applies only to the first person singular and plural: "I" and "we". For the second and third persons the practice is **will** for the ordinary future sense, and **shall** for the idea of obligation= "must". "After this incident he shall never enter my house again." "Thou shalt not steal." "Nor shall my sword sleep in my hand."

An example of misuse often given in grammar books is that of the drowning man calling out: "I will be drowned;

nobody shall save me". This person is represented as an Irishman, and laxity in the use of the words was formerly said to be especially a sign of the Scottish and Irish, but today all over the British Isles and the Commonwealth the use in the first person of **shall** and even more of **should** threatens to become as obsolete in this country as it is in America. Those who still preserve the distinction will regard its disappearance as an impoverishment of the language.

Perhaps the neglect of the distinction between **shall** and **will**, and between **should** and **would**, is connected with the increasing use of the contractions **I'll, We'll, I'd, We'd.**

An exception to the use of **would** in the first person to imply wishing, etc., is its use to denote habitual action: "Often when I passed the house I would see her working in the garden".

329   SHAMBLES, SLAUGHTER-HOUSE

Till recently both words meant a place where cattle are killed for meat. **shambles** was used also for a scene of carnage where human beings have been killed in large numbers. Today **shambles** is a favourite word in journalese, not for scenes of slaughter and blood, but for material wreckage, especially that of houses and rooms. Thus if in the absence of the occupiers, and so without injury to living creatures, a house were destroyed by fire a newspaper reporter might describe the scene of havoc as a **shambles**.

330   SHIP, BOAT, VESSEL

The word **boat** is generally used for a small rowing or sailing craft, or for a small steamer. Even a large liner, however, can be so called ("We caught the boat at Marseilles"), though it would not be by a sailor. There is also the term **boat-train,** which runs to and from the side of a steamship.

ship is a word for any craft larger than a **boat** in its general sense as defined above.

vessel is a formal word (see 15).

SHORT, BRIEF, CONCISE   331

The ordinary working words are **short, brief, concise**.

The following table shows the main similarities and differences in the use of the five words.

Can be applied to

speaker	——	——	concise	succinct	——
writer	——	——	concise	succinct	terse
speech	short*	brief*	concise	succinct	terse
writing	short	brief	concise	succinct	terse

There are two nouns corresponding to **concise: conciseness** and **concision. conciseness** is the working word used. **concision** belongs to the class of words *M.E.U.* calls "Literary Critics' Words," of which, the better the critic is, the fewer he uses.

SHOW-DOWN, TEST   332

In the American card game poker a player declares his hand by laying down his cards with faces up. This is technically called a **show-down**. Figuratively a **show-down** is a "final **test**, disclosure of achievements or possibilities" (*C.O.D.*), but the word is coming into frequent use as a synonym of "trial of strength" ("Hitler was obviously determined to have a show-down over Poland that year"), or even for a private "row".

SHUT, CLOSE   333

Fowler classes **close**, instead of **shut**, as both a formal word (see 15) and a genteelism (see 34), citing "close the door (or window)". This seems far-fetched, though perhaps

* In dimensions of time.

shut is the more common word. The notice on a gate in a field or elsewhere would almost certainly be "Shut this gate". Nevertheless "the doctor gave orders that the windows should be kept closed" is surely as straightforward and ordinary as if the word used were **shut**.

In figurative senses **close** is more idiomatic than **shut**. "My club is always closed for a fortnight in August." Nor is **shut** used in the sense of "bring to an end" as **close** is: "He closed the discussion".

334   SINCERELY, TRULY, FAITHFULLY

Until recent years **truly** (or **very truly**) served for the halfway point between the formality of **faithfully** and the intimacy of **sincerely** (or **very sincerely**). **faithfully** at the end of a letter would follow "Sir", "Dear Sir", "Madam", "Dear Madam", at the beginning; whereas **sincerely** would follow "Dear Mr. . . .", "Dear Mrs. . . .", etc.; and **truly** might follow either (1) or (2). Today **truly** has almost disappeared, and even a person one has not met, but with whom one is in correspondence, may in his very first letter address one as "Dear Mr. . . ." and sign himself "Yours sincerely".

Rules of etiquette prescribe how one should address persons of rank. To and from one of His Majesty's Ministers the formal signature is "Your obedient servant", and some government departments still so sign letters to even the smallest fry. **faithfully**, however, is today replacing this habit, and it can be used to serve all purposes outside letters to friends and social acquaintances. When one is in doubt it is safer to be "faithful" than "sincere".

335   SLOGAN, WATCHWORD, MOTTO, CATCHWORD

In their synonymous use these words mean a saying adopted as a guiding principle: e.g. "Small Profits, Quick

Returns"; "Safety First"; "Guns before Butter". **slogan**
and **watchword** have a military origin: **slogan** was originally
a Highland war-cry; **watchword** a military password.
Today **slogan** refers especially to the expression, for purposes of propaganda, of the principles of a body of people:
e.g. a political party. **motto** is generally used for a maxim of
ideal conduct. Thus "Manners makyth man" is the **motto**
of Winchester College; *Per ardua ad astra*, of the R.A.F.
catchword has generally a somewhat contemptuous ring for
what is regarded as a vague or sophistic or misleading or
insincere expression of principle.

SMELL, ODOUR, SCENT, PERFUME, 336
FRAGRANCE, AROMA, BOUQUET

A general distinction between these words is that **smell**
and **odour** can imply what is either pleasant or unpleasant,
whereas all the other words always imply what is pleasant
except **scent** in a special use, in hunting, for the "trail", left
by a creature, that is perceptible to dogs.

smell is the working word. **odour** is on the formal side
(see 15) except in the metaphorical phrases "in bad odour",
"the odour of sanctity". **scent** and **perfume** are the most
common words for a **smell** that is pleasant. **perfume**, in spite
of its honourable history, its poetical associations ("All the
perfumes of Arabia will not sweeten this little hand"), and
its euphony, is somewhat of a genteelism (see 85). **fragrance** (generally of flowers) is closely synonymous with
scent and **perfume**, but is not used so much. **aroma** is a
show-word except when applied to a few things: e.g. coffee,
a cigar. **bouquet** is restricted to the **fragrance** of wine.

scent and **perfume** mean also the liquid distilled from
flowers or manufactured synthetically, and in this sense too
perfume is a genteelism or trade word used in shops or by
the "perfumery" trade.

In their roughly synonymous meanings all these words imply misuse in language, but **mistake** and **error** (for which see also 208) are also words of general application.

solecism is a **mistake, error**, made in grammar, idiom or pronunciation. (It is sometimes used also of a breach of manners.)

jargon is defined by *C.O.D.* in its first meaning as "unintelligible words, gibberish". More precisely it refers to technical words and phrases used in particular industries, trades, professions, etc., especially when introduced into ordinary speech and writing. It is sometimes used also for language that is circumlocutory, or that chooses abstract, or what Quiller-Couch calls "woolly", rather than concrete, nouns.

catachresis is grammarians' **jargon** for the wrong use of a word.

A **howler** is a colloquialism for a glaring blunder in grammar, statements of fact, interpretation, definition, etc., mostly used with reference to schoolboys' mistakes.

338   BE SORRY, BE AFRAID, FEAR, REGRET

To be **sorry** and to be **afraid** might seem to have no synonymous relation to each other, for strictly used they imply widely different emotions. Nevertheless the expression "I am afraid" (or "I fear") is often used when the meaning is "I am sorry" and the speaker or writer has neither fear nor anxiety about anything. (1) Customer: "Have you any lemons?" Greengrocer (quite conversant with his stock, and without any intention to examine it): "I am afraid I have none." (2) A: "Can I look at your *Bradshaw*?" B: "I am afraid I have not a copy." (3) A: "Do you greatly admire Gide's work?" "I am afraid I have not read any." (4)—in a letter—"I am therefore afraid I cannot accept your offer." (5)—in a letter—"I fear we must decline to enter into any further discussion of the matter." The idiom is an ellipsis. The meaning is "I am afraid you will be disappointed to hear that I have none", etc. The intention is polite, but why not—more simply, directly, precisely, and truthfully—"I am sorry", "I regret"?

SPECIALLY, ESPECIALLY, PARTICULARLY 339

As concisely formulated by Treble and Vallins in *An ABC of English Usage*, **especially** means "to an exceptional degree", **specially** "for one purpose and no other". "The weather has been especially cold lately;" but "I came specially to see you".

particularly is used in the sense of both words, and could be substituted for either in these two sentences.

The adjective **especial** is not used much.

SPEECH, HARANGUE, TIRADE 340

An **harangue** is primarily "a speech made to an assembly", but the word has come to mean a **speech** that is vehement, and, generally, vulgarly expressed: e.g. by a tub-thumping orator in Hyde Park. A **tirade** also means a **speech** of this style, but not necessarily addressed to a number of people: it can be made privately to one person.

SPOT, PIECE 341

spot has for some time been used colloquially for **piece, bit, small amount**, etc., but is now beginning to appear in journalese. It is often applied to abstract as well as to concrete things, so that, besides "a spot of lunch" or "a spot of whisky", one may now hear of a "spot of work" or "a spot of trouble".

The established meaning today of the verb **stage** is "put (a play) on the stage". I am indebted to the late Earl Wavell for the information that **stage** has also for long been recognized as a term for making the necessary arrangements in military operations, corresponding in use to a somewhat later term **mount**. The entry of **stage** in the *Shorter Oxford English Dictionary* gives, besides "put on the stage", several uses that are now obsolete except one with the meaning of exhibiting flowers on a raised structure. The word, however, has in recent years become a wearisomely frequent vogue-word (see 34) as a substitute for **arrange, organize, plan, carry out, perform**, etc. References to games are especially rich in the word. We read that "no competitive event in sport has been staged between England and Germany since the war"; tennis championships are no longer **played**, but are **staged**, at Wimbledon, and football finals at Wembley. It is not only the journalistic world that has become stage-struck. A government department announces that trials of certain offenders will be **staged** as quickly as possible. We are told by the B.B.C. that arrangements for a Moscow conference are being **staged**. A politician says "There is no country where it is harder to stage a coalition than Greece," and a historian that "Time alone will show whether Europe can stage an economic recovery".

Apart from its use in a theatrical or military sense, as mentioned in the first two sentences, the word is best reserved for the sense of a planned demonstration. "On November 30th the Fascists **staged** in the Italian Parliament a scene of shouted claims against France."

343   STAGGER, SPREAD

For some years **stagger** has been used as a synonym of **spread** with reference to holidays or the periods within which employees are engaged in work. Arrangements **are**

made so that some businesses open and close at different
times from others, or that employees enter and leave in
batches at intervals instead of all at the same time, and
have their holidays at different times. Gardeners use
stagger for the method of arranging plants in parallel rows
in such a way that the individual plants are not exactly
opposite one another. (Compare **echelon** in military operations.) These uses of the word are of American origin and
fairly recent introduction here but are by now firmly
established.

STEAL, PURLOIN, PILFER, FILCH, THIEVE, ROB 344

steal is the working word for taking something to which
one has no right. **purloin** is a formal word (see 15). **pilfer**
and **filch** refer to a petty theft. **thieve** is seldom used transitively. **rob** is sometimes used as a synonym of **steal** in an
incorrect construction: "He robbed a thousand pounds."
A thief can "rob a victim of a thousand pounds", and can
"rob a bank", but cannot be said to rob what the victim or
the bank has.

STEP UP, INCREASE   345

step up for **increase** is one of the recent combinations of
verbs with prepositions of adverbial force. It was primarily
an American term used in engineering for gradually increasing the power applied by a switch with graduated "steps"
or "stations". Over here it has spread from journalese to
Whitehall. During the war we were told that the Government were anxious to "step up the collection of waste
paper", and more recently that "It is now possible to step
up quantities of coal for certain industries". For the principle involved in formations of this sort see 196. **step up**
may come to have a distinctive meaning with reference to
something that is made greater by stages. Otherwise, as
merely a substitute for **increase**, it is a superfluous addition
to the language.

A **stimulus** (Latin="goad") is the general word for something that rouses to activity. A **stimulant** is more commonly used for food (especially alcoholic drink) or drugs that have an exciting effect, though figurative uses are to be found: e.g. "Virtuous indignation is a powerful stimulant" (Bernard Shaw).

347 STOIC, STOICAL

These words apply to the philosophy of Stoicism, founded by the Greek Zeno, with its inculcation of the control of the passions and of indifference to pleasure and pain. As Treble and Vallins's *ABC of English Usage* points out, **stoic** is used when the reference is directly or indirectly to the philosophy itself: "a stoic philosopher", "He showed stoic indifference". **stoical** is used in a more general sense (usually qualifying persons only): "a stoical sufferer".

348 STOMACH, BELLY, ABDOMEN, TUMMY

stomach (French *estomac*) is the word generally used for the whole of the human body lying between the breast and the thighs, and in particular is regarded as the region where food is digested. Strictly the **stomach** is only a part of this region, medically called the **abdomen**, which is the whole cavity of the body, containing stomach, bowels and other organs; nor is the process of digestion confined to the **stomach**. Fowler classes **stomach** as a genteelism (see 85) for **belly**, which is a strict synonym of **abdomen**. **belly** (Saxon: the same word, originally meaning "bag," of which the plural appears in "bellows") is used at least thirty times in the Bible: e.g. in the parable of the Prodigal Son, who (Authorized Version) "would fain have filled his belly with the husks that the swine did eat", and in the "Song of Solomon", in which both the man and the woman praise the **belly** of the beloved. In the early Victorian age the word came to be banned as improper. When William Cory wrote the "Eton Boating Song", the refrain seems to have been originally "Pull, pull together, with your bellies between your knees". When, however, in 1865, the song was printed in the *Eton Scrap Book*, Cory altered, or was prevailed on to acquiesce in the editor's altering, this to the absurd and unmetrical "with your backs between your knees". (I am indebted for this information to Mrs. Faith Compton Mackenzie.) The word used now in singing the song at Eton is, I am told, "bodies". Even to those not affected by gentility **belly** has today almost an archaic air, though a parent anxious to uphold the cause of pure English undefiled can feel he has sound literary grounds for being linguistically sympathetic if he overhears Tommy telling Joan that he has a **belly-ache**.

The most genteel of all shy even at **stomach**, and are not ashamed to use the nursery-word **tummy**.

STOP, END, FINISH, CEASE, TERMINATE, 349 CONCLUDE, DISCONTINUE, DESIST, INTERMIT, COMPLETE

desist (from) is intransitive; the other words both transitive and intransitive.

stop, end and **finish** are the ordinary working words.

end and **finish** have more strongly than **stop** and the other words the sense of finality. "This ended our quarrel." "The war ended in 1945." "That finished the matter." On the other hand "The children stopped their game to look at the procession", but they may have returned to the game; and "The rain has stopped", but it may come on again. Another distinction is that **end** is not idiomatically followed by a gerund. For "He stopped writing to me", "Have you finished reading that book?" the substitution of ended would not be idiomatic.

cease in conversation would be pompous: e.g. "I must

now cease work for the day", or "The rain has ceased"; and Sir Harry Lauder's song, "Stop your tickling, Jock", would not run so naturally with "cease". *M.E.U.* considers **cease**, except when used poetically, an old-fashioned word that should be allowed to go into honourable retirement, but it is still often used in prose by good writers. Moreover it is useful with an infinitive: 'Further help from him ceased to be necessary".

terminate and **conclude** are formal words (see 15).

To **discontinue** generally implies to **stop** doing something one has been doing for some time or is in the habit of doing. "I will discontinue my subscription". "She discontinued her weekly visits".

To **desist** is generally used with reference to abandoning some course of action. "As I saw he was so exhausted I desisted from asking him any more questions."

To **intermit** is to "bring to an end for a time", to "suspend".

For nouns see 88.

350   STRESS, EMPHASIZE

The verb **stress** has a long history. As far back as the sixteenth century it meant to "subject a person to force". It had also a scientific use. It then came to be used in the sense of **emphasize** with reference to a syllable, word, or phrase in speaking, or to a syllable in poetical composition. Similarly the noun came to be used in prosody: e.g. "strong stress", "weak stress". This use of the verb, and of the noun (generally in the phrase "lay stress on"), has been extended to apply to facts and ideas. A speaker or a writer is said, with reference to something, to **stress** its importance, difficulty, seriousness, need, advantage, cheapness. In this sense the verb has become a vogue-word (see 34). Sir Ernest Gowers, in *Plain Words*, deprecates its being overworked when **emphasize** is available.

superlative in its primary sense means "of the highest degree". As idiomatically it refers to what is admirable (e.g. "superlative beauty or wisdom", but hardly "superlative ugliness or folly"), it comes to be synonymous with **excellent, perfect**, etc. Its application should be restricted to qualities, and not applied to people and acts: "superlative eloquence", not a "superlative speaker, actor, play, pass (in football)". An obituary notice described the novelist A. E. Mason as a "superlative storyteller", which is journalese, and then properly as "a craftsman of superlative skill".

The adverb **superlatively** also is applied to qualities that are admirable: "superlatively kind", "superlatively mean". In this way **superlative** and **superlatively** are in contrast with **excessive** and **excessively** (see 104), which are always applied to what is not admirable.

A contraction of **superlative** to **super** has produced such horrors as "a super cinema" and "This is super".

SUPPLEMENTARY, COMPLEMENTARY,   352
ADDITIONAL

The words, implying increase in number or quality, could be in some contexts interchanged. **supplementary**, however, is used for emphasizing that what is added supplies something lacking in a previous arrangement: "He was granted three additional days on leave"; "I have made some additional corrections in the book"; but "In the new edition of the book a supplementary chapter covers the latest developments in this branch of the science"; "A supplementary estimate was drawn up to provide for those items". **complementary** has the further implication that the addition is essential and makes something complete, but it is seldom used except in a technical sense: e.g. in mathematics for two angles making up 90 degrees.

353 SURRENDER, ASTONISH, AMAZE, ASTOUND

The words as given above are in ascending order of the degree of emotion roused by the unexpected. **astound** often carries with it the further idea of "shock", "profoundly disturb".

354 SURRENDER, CAPITULATE

surrender can be used with reference to the ending of (*a*) physical resistance, especially in war, (*b*) other forms of resistance: e.g. one can **surrender** a claim, or **surrender** in argument. **capitulate** is generally used only in sense (*a*) for the end of military resistance. By etymology **capitulate** means "draw up an agreement under heads" (Latin *capita*=heads), and *C.O.D.* defines it in its military sense as "surrender on terms".

355 SUSPENSION, SUSPENSE

Both words are related to the verb **suspend**, which by derivation and in its primary, literal sense means "hang up between two points". **suspension** in its figurative sense, with reference to the mind, means that one's judgment is temporarily "hung up", "held up", "in abeyance". **suspense** in its common use means a state of anxiety in waiting for some event or news. In the phrase, however, "suspense of judgment" it has the meaning of **suspension**, and here only are the words synonymous.

356 SUSTAIN, SUFFER

sustain, by derivation (Latin *sustinere*) and in its primary sense, means "bear the weight of", materially "support"; thence figuratively "support with the mind," "endure". In a further extension it has come to be a show-word (see 15), with reference to a loss or other unpleasant experience, as a synonym of **suffer**. In this jargon an army is said to "sustain a defeat"; a person, "sustain a disappointment"; the victims of street and other accidents, "sustain injuries".

SWEAT, PERSPIRATION   357

sweat is used in the Bible: e.g. "In the sweat of thy face shalt thou eat bread", "His sweat was as it were great drops of blood"; in the Prayer Book: "agony and bloody sweat"; in Shakespeare: "Falstaff shall die of a sweat"; and throughout literature. In the Victorian age, however, a well-known principal of a college used to tell her students "Horses sweat, men perspire, but young ladies come all of a glow." Nearly thirty years ago Fowler classed **perspiration** as a genteelism. Today with greater freedom in language there are probably not many households where **sweat** would be thought an unsuitable word, especially since Mr. Winston Churchill's famous speech in 1940, on taking office as Prime Minister, when in the House of Commons he told the nation what struggles and sufferings lay before it: "I have nothing to offer but blood, toil, tears and sweat".

SYNTHETIC, ARTIFICIAL, IMITATION,   358
ERSATZ

synthetic is generally used with reference to the production of chemical compounds from their constituents (e.g. "synthetic rubber", "synthetic indigo") as opposed to their extract from plants, etc. What in this sense is **synthetic** is often called, instead, **artificial** or (in its adjectival use) **imitation**: e.g. "artificial rubber", "imitation pearls". **artificial** is generally used for something that has a practical purpose: e.g. "artificial teeth, leg, light". **imitation** has not this implication. Thus "imitation pearls" have only an ornamental purpose. Thus also in the play *R.U.R.* the robots are **artificial** human beings, performing human functions, whereas in a tailor's window the dummies are **imitation** figures of human beings. Idiom, however, is often fluid, and one would ask in a shop for "artificial" not "imitation" flowers. **ersatz** (German) has in recent years come into use as an epithet for a thing that is a substitute: e.g. ground acorns for coffee.

359   TALK, CONVERSATION, CONVERSE, DISCOURSE

talk, rather than **conversation**, would generally be preferred for an informal or short communication, especially between not more than two persons; otherwise **conversation** would probably be used. There is, however, an idiomatic use where **conversation** is always used: one "gets into conversation" with a person. Moreover the use in broadcasting of **talk** as equivalent to **lecture** ("At 7 p.m. Mr. A. will give a talk on Spain") is causing **conversation** to become the ordinary word for speech between persons.

converse, both as a verb and as a noun, is archaic. So too is **discourse**, in the general sense of having a **talk** with someone, but it is still used with reference to "holding forth" in speech or writing.

360   TALL, HIGH, LOFTY

tall tends to be used for that which is thought of primarily with reference to its perpendicular elevation. It carries with it the idea of slenderness, slimness: e.g. a "tall girl, goblet, spire"; "My sweet peas have grown unusually tall this year". On the other hand **high** tends to be used where, besides perpendicular elevation, there is an idea of bigness: a "high table, house, mountain". Nevertheless the distinction is not hard and fast. Thus a well-grown tree can be thought of as both **tall** and **high**; a wall is **high** rather than **tall** (perhaps for euphony); and idiom requires one to ride, both literally and metaphorically, a horse that is **high**. **lofty** (e.g. of a ceiling, a mountain) emphasizes still more strongly, in something that could also be called **high,** the idea of bigness, of space covered. It is used also metaphorically: e.g. "lofty contempt".

tall, colloquially, means also "excessive", "exorbitant", "unreasonable" ("That is a tall order"), and "boastful" ("tall talk", or, adverbially, "to talk tall").

TARGET, OBJECTIVE 361

target, used for an **objective** to be reached, with reference to a result expressed in numerical terms (e.g. a given amount in material production) is probably the most common of recently introduced vogue-words (see 34).

A **target** is primarily a stuffed pad with concentric circles painted on the surface as a mark in archery and for rifles or pistols, with an established figurative use, applied to a person, as a mark for scorn, etc. In an extension of its literal meaning, from that of a single weapon directing a missile at a mark, to a more general meaning, it can serve a useful purpose. "Some military critics consider that for the initial stroke of the Japanese in the last war the Panama Canal would have been a better target than Pearl Harbour." "The immediate target in the firm's present policy is the colonial market." Used, however, in a numerical application it is at best not a happy metaphor, because no idea of numbers is involved in the original meaning of the word. Moreover in such a phrase as "the coal target" the relation between coal and **target** cannot be the same as that between a rifle and a **target.** The metaphor becomes increasingly awkward and even absurd when one is told that a certain result (e.g. in exported goods or small savings) is "above the target" or "beyond the target", for if a shot goes above or beyond a **target** it fails to achieve its object. Again, as *The Times* has pointed out in an amusing Fourth Leader, when a Minister talks of efforts to "increase the target", it is difficult not to reflect that, the bigger a **target** is, the easier it is to hit; and, as for raising the **target,** that it is only when a **target** is lowered that it becomes more difficult and finally impossible to hit. In two of the latest extensions of the metaphor we have been told that it is "the duty of industry to take a national target-figure and break it down", and, in the dimension of time, that in the production of coal we are "a week behind the target".

The word in this metaphorical sense is also being used adjectivally: "Our target date was September 19th".

362   TELL, INFORM, ADVISE, ACQUAINT, APPRISE

For the meaning "make known," **tell** is the working word.

As a substitute for **tell** in letters **inform** is officialese and commercialese. "We have to inform you that on the return of the enclosed form filled up your application will be considered." "We will inform you when the goods are ready to be dispatched." For announcements of importance, however, in formal circumstances, **inform** can be more suitable than **tell**. When, e.g. in Parliament, a Minister says "I am informed that the risk to the public is remote", the use of the verb **tell** would have struck too colloquial a note, for "I am told" is a phrase often used in conversation with reference to something one has heard more or less idly said. **informed** in a Minister's statement implies that he has received his "information" from authoritative sources.

advise, as a substitute for **tell**, is a purposeless extension in officialese and commercialese of a word that in its established use has a distinctive and useful meaning ("give advice," "give counsel"). The noun **advices** also is used in officialese for **information, news**. "I am to advise you that the matter is under consideration." "We wish to advise you of the following reductions in our prices."

acquaint has today an archaic air.

apprise and **intimate** are formal words. **intimate** is used for information conveyed in an indirect way: equivalent to the common phrase "give to understand."

The relative pronoun **that** is often—one might perhaps say generally—regarded only as a closely synonymous variant of **which**. Grammar, however, distinguishes between "defining" ("restrictive") and non-defining ("non-restrictive") adjectival clauses.

A defining adjectival clause, says Fowler in *M.E.U.*, "identifies the person or thing meant by limiting the denotation of the antecedent". He illustrates this by the sentence "Each made a list of books that had influenced him," and adds "not books generally, but books as defined by the that-clause". He then contrasts this with the sentence "I always buy his books, which have influenced me greatly," and adds "The clause does not limit 'his books', for they need no limitation: it gives a reason ('for they have'), or a new fact ('and they have')".

If there is doubt whether a clause is defining or non-defining a reliable test can generally be made by considering whether a comma after the antecedent is natural and desirable. If it is, the clause is generally non-defining; otherwise it is defining. Thus nobody would think of having a comma after "house" in "This is the house that Jack built". In the opinion of Mr. G. V. Carey, author of an excellent book on punctuation, *Mind the Stop*, it is even more important to differentiate between the two types of clause by the omission or insertion of a comma than by the use of **that** as contrasted with the use of **which**.

Addison nearly two hundred years ago wrote an essay about the "Humble Petition of Who and Which", where these words complained of being supplanted from their ancient dignity and honour till the Jacksprat **that** supplanted them. Addison was historically wrong; **that** as a relative pronoun is much older than **who, whom, which**. Since Addison's day **which** has encroached on **that**. When Morley wrote his *Life of Gladstone* he asked a friend to read his manuscript and do some "which hunting" for him. It is to be noted that Morley said nothing about hunting for

who and **whom**. Fowler himself, while strongly advocating the observance of a distinction, in the use of the relative pronouns, between defining and non-defining clauses, says the use of **that** referring to persons is apt today to sound archaic except when the antecedent is **it** or has attached to it a superlative or other word of exclusive meaning. "It was you that said so"; "the most impartial critic that could be found"; but "A person who desires to be popular in society must be amiable".

There is one objection to the rigid use of **that** in defining clauses. **that**, besides being a relative pronoun, is also a demonstrative pronoun and a conjunction. Consequently there are some occasions when more than one **that**, with different functions, might be jostling one another in the same sentence with harm to euphony. A solution of the difficulty can be to use a construction dispensing with a relative pronoun: "That is the house we occupied when first we moved to London"; or, by means of a past participle, "That is the house occupied by us . . ."

Fowler says that if the vital difference between a defining and a non-defining clause were consistently marked, wherever it is possible, by a discriminating use of **that** and **which**, false co-ordinating and other mishandlings of the relation would be less common than they are. He has to admit that many writers, including some of the best, pay no attention to the distinction. Many speakers and writers hardly ever use **that** as a relative pronoun. Others regard **that** and **which** as now entirely synonymous. Others again maintain that the decisive consideration in a given instance is not sense but euphony. In the present book the distinction has always been preserved as a nice and useful one.

364   THEIR, HIS, HER

A most common use is that of the pronominal adjective **their**, which stands for "of them" (plural), with reference to a subject that is singular, especially indefinite or distributive pronouns like "anyone", "everyone", "everybody", "each", "nobody:" e.g. "Everybody naturally ranks their own country first". There are some to defend this usage on the grounds that English has no singular possessive adjective to mean both **his** and **her**, and that therefore in the sentence given above the only alternative to **their**, covering both sexes, would be the clumsy **his or her**. Who would imagine however, that "his own country" referred only to men and not also to women? Others argue that, although **everyone** is singular in form, it is in the minds of the user plural. Nevertheless those arguing thus do not use a singular verb after these pronouns, and would not say or write "Everyone naturally rank their own country first".

If rightly one refuses to have any truck with the ungrammatical **their**, not unreasonably deprecates the cumbrousness of **his and her**, **his or her**, and yet refuses to let **his** be used to cover both sexes, the only solution is to remodel the sentence so as to avoid the embarrassing pronouns: e.g. by the use of **all** instead of **anyone** or **everyone**.

none: since **none**="not one," logical grammar would fix it as singular, like **no one**, but recognized idiom often treats it as plural: e.g. "None of the soldiers have yet come", and correspondingly, "None of the soldiers had been able to save their equipment".

THINK, CONSIDER, FEEL   365

feel is often used loosely as a synonym for **think** and **consider**, meaning "be of opinion", "believe". "I feel his conduct was outrageous." "I feel it would be unwise to accept the offer." The usage is not only colloquial. Thus in a report of an important international conference we read that "The British delegate said he felt this course would be dangerous". The nearest sense in which **feel** can properly get to that of **think** and **consider** is "have a vague or emotional conviction" (*C.O.D.*). Sir Ernest Gowers in *Plain*

Words reminds government departments that **thinking** is a rational process, **feeling** is an intuitive one; and that official decisions should not be described as the products of intuition, however they may actually have been arrived at.

366   THRASH, BEAT, BEAT UP

As an addition to the large number of words meaning to "inflict blows on", **beat** (the common working word), **thrash, chastise**, etc., there has come into use recently the combination **beat up**, which already had several established and distinctive meanings, including that of rousing game to make them a mark for the shooter. If this use is restricted, as it seems to have been when first it was introduced, to imply an assault, generally on a political opponent, that has been organized, something may be said for it, but when it is used as a substitute for **beat** in its ordinary sense, the **up** is mere verbosity: "The girl said she could only remember being beaten up and thrown out of the car".

367   THROW, CAST

cast has had a long and honourable history, both literally and especially figuratively. "Let him first cast a stone at her;" "Cast not your pearls before swine;" "nor cast one longing lingering look behind". It still survives in many common idioms. We **cast** lots, votes, an anchor, a net, a line, a column of figures, a horoscope; deer **cast** their horns and snakes their skins; actors are **cast** for parts; we **cast** aside scruples, and **cast** aspersions. Today, however, though apart from these idioms the word might be used in poetry, it would be pompous if used for ordinary purposes instead of **throw**: e.g. with reference to a ball, litter into a bin, a bone to a dog, a letter into the fire.

throw too has its idiomatic uses. Thus we **throw** a veil over a distressing incident; we **throw** something disagreeable in the teeth of our opponent; we **throw** off disguises and even verses.

top is the working word. **summit**, in its literal sense, is generally restricted to the highest point in rising ground: e.g. of a mountain. **peak** is the highest point of something that is pointed, especially a mountain. **apex** is generally restricted to its mathematical use for the vertex of a triangle or cone. All four words are used figuratively (**apex** less than the others): e.g. "top of the school", "summit of his power", "peak of his ambitions", "apex of his fortunes". **peak** has a special use, as a highest point, with reference to a series of rises or fluctuations, e.g. "peak-period in traffic", "peak of electric power".

TOWARDS, TOWARD   369

towards today is the prevailing form. **toward** is generally restricted to poetry. In U.S.A. **toward** is nearly always used.

TRANSPORT, TRANSPORTATION   370

In the past the word **transportation** was familiar in the term "transportation for life" for the removal of a criminal to a penal colony. Today **transportation** and **transport** are closely synonymous for the taking of goods and persons from one place to another, and there is no point in using four syllables instead of two. Fortunately the love of long words has stopped short of using "Transportation Workers" for the name of the trade union, and of the title "Minister of Transportation".

TRICK, MANŒUVRE, STRATAGEM,   371
SUBTERFUGE

All these words mean a method of gaining one's end by deceiving an opponent. (**manœuvre** is primarily a military or naval term.) **subterfuge** is generally used in a bad sense, for a device that employs dishonourable means. The other words can have a bad or neutral implication according to the context. So can the verb **manœuvre**, but the verb **trick**, like the noun **trickster**, always has a bad sense.

372   TRIUMPHANT, TRIUMPHAL

triumphant refers (1) to a person who is brilliantly successful; (2) to a person who is elated with his success; (3) to the success itself. Thus (1) "Wellington was triumphant at Waterloo." (2) "The inventor was triumphant over the results of his experiment." (3) "The use of penicillin in many diseases has been a triumphant success."

triumphal cannot be applied to persons. It refers to a procession or similar celebration, or the erection of a building: e.g. a "triumphal arch", in honour of a brilliant success, originally used of an arch set up in classical times, through which a procession passed in celebration of a Roman military triumph.

373   TRY, TRY OUT, TEST, TEST OUT

To **try out** and (rarer) to **test out**, as synonyms of to **try**, to **test**, are among the most common recent introductions of verbs combined with prepositions of adverbial force (see 196). The Oxford dictionaries do not give to **test out**. In their treatment of to **try out** they vary. *C.O.D.* gives it, but neither the *Oxford English Dictionary* nor the *Shorter Oxford English Dictionary*. There is, however, authority for it in the Book of Common Prayer, Psalm XXVI, 2: "Try out my reins and my heart". This is based on Cranmer's translation of the Bible; the Authorized and the Revised Versions have **try**. To **try out** and its noun (see below) may become established with the sense of making a test that is thorough—over a considerable period of time, on a considerable scale, etc.: e.g. "A fair body of opinion is in favour of comprehensive schools. The experiment is bound to take time, but to try them out is good sense".

The noun **try out** (given by *C.O.D.*, but not by *O.E.D.* and *S.O.E.D.*), as a synonym of **test, try, trial**, is also now common. Sometimes in an official document it will be found typed or printed within inverted commas—a weak compromise, for it is sounder either, if a word is thought to be useful and to serve a distinctive meaning, to use it boldly, without shamefacedness or implied apology, or not to use it at all.

In engineering **try out,** both verb and noun, is often used with reference to the **trial** or **test** of a composite body—e.g. of a motor-car—of which the component parts have been individually **tried** or **tested** before assembly.

TYPIST, TYPEWRITER   374

When typewriting was first introduced the word **typewriter** served both for the machine and its user. Since **typist**, at first colloquial, has come into general use, **typewriter** ought to be restricted to the machine.

UNDERSTAND, COMPREHEND, APPREHEND   375

comprehend and **apprehend** are show-words (see 15) for **understand**.

apprehend is used also by the sham-erudite as a synonym of **arrest** and of **fear**.

UNDOUBTEDLY, DOUBTLESS, INDUBITABLY   376

undoubtedly is the working word. **doubtless** in some contexts might imply that the speaker or writer is making a concession in the course of a statement or argument: equivalent to "I admit that". **indubitably** is a pretentious substitute for these two words. It dies hard. In the last century Sir John Hare in Robertson's comedies was given to make fun of it, as does Sir Max Beerbohm in a parody of Henry James: "They so very indubitably *are*, you know".

"due" means, primarily, "owing", "payable" ("The second instalment was now due"); secondarily, "suitable", "adequate", etc. ("The task was begun with due precautions"). Parallel with the secondary meaning, **undue**, its opposite, is used in such a statement as "He regarded this slight setback with undue concern:" i.e. concern that was **excessive, unnecessary, unjustified**; similarly the adverb: "He was unduly alarmed". In loose extensions, however, the words are often used with gross tautology. "There is no reason for undue concern." "You need not be unduly concerned." Unless the meanings of the words are to be watered down to become merely unnecessary substitutes for "great", "greatly", etc., these statements can only mean "There is no reason for concern for which there is no reason". Typical of still worse usage: "Bengal has worked out its destiny since partition without undue violence". What, then, is the amount of murder and rapine that was **due**?

378   UNILATERAL, INDEPENDENT

unilateral can be a useful word to denote action taken by a party to an agreement, in violation of an undertaking that one side shall not move in a particular matter without the consent of or consultation with the other side. Owing to conditions today in international politics, especially the relations between the Great Powers since the end of the war, the word has come into frequent use, but its sense is now being extended to cover the idea of merely **independent** action when there does not exist an agreement.

379   UNIQUE, SINGULAR, EXCEPTIONAL

unique (derived, through the French *unique*, from the Latin *unicus*, adjective of *unus*=one) means **unmatched, unequalled**, "having in some respects no like or equal or parallel", "one and only". Its correct use is therefore restricted to a sole existing specimen. A thing can be "nearly" or "almost" **unique**, or even, though redundantly, "quite unique"; it cannot be "very", "most", "rather", "comparatively", etc., **unique**, as there are no degrees of uniqueness.

singular in its primary meaning is synonymous with **unique**, and as such cannot be qualified by "very", "most". It is not, however, now often so used, and (apart from its grammatical use, for the **singular**, as opposed to the **plural**, number) has merely the meaning of **unusual, rare, remarkable, strange, odd**, etc., as have its noun **singularity** and adverb **singularly**. Mr. Raymond Mortimer attributes the popularity of the words in this sense to Lytton Strachey, "who liked using the word to denote oddity".

exceptional ("forming an exception") could logically be synonymous with **unique**, if only one exception were involved, but it is generally used, like **singular**, for **unusual**, etc.

UNSOPHISTICATED, INEXPERIENCED, 380
NAIVE, ARTLESS

unsophisticated refers to a person's general unfamiliarity with worldly affairs, especially with the behaviour of human beings in society. **inexperienced** can also be used in this general sense, but it usually refers to a person who, through never having been engaged in a given occupation or other activity, has no practical knowledge of it. **naive** is close in sense to **unsophisticated**, with an additional implication that a person's character and conduct are so simple and candid as to be amusing. **artless** (free from "art" in the sense of "artifice", without "artificiality") also means simple in character and conduct, often with a slightly depreciatory implication of tactlessness or clumsiness.

UNTHINKABLE, INCONCEIVABLE 381

unthinkable and **inconceivable** in their proper meanings for what is "unable to be imagined" or what "reason declares to be impossible" are closely synonymous. **unthinkable**, however, is used in loose extensions to mean merely "extremely remarkable", "almost passing belief", or merely "unlikely". Compare **impossible** (153).

382 USE, USAGE

use is the ordinary working noun. "Can you make use of this?" "That machine has been out of use a long time." **usage** has an additional implication of the manner in which a person or thing is treated, especially (*a*) in a bad sense: "He was subjected to rough usage"; (*b*) with reference to practice in speaking and writing: e.g. we speak of the **usage** of the best writers, and the present book has constantly referred to Fowler's *Dictionary of Modern English Usage*.

383 VARIOUS, VARIED

varied (past participle of the verb **vary**, used as an adjective) and **various**, when it is used with a plural noun, mean "of different kinds", and in many contexts could be interchanged. "Interpretations of this poem are varied (or various)". In another sense **various** is sometimes used as synonymous with "several" (which implies "not many": see 114) or "many." This leads to ambiguity. "I have come across him in recent years on various occasions." Three or four? Dozens? Hundreds? A precise speaker or writer will avoid this use of the word.

384 VENUE, MEETING-PLACE

venue (strictly a legal term for the place appointed for a jury trial) is a show-word (see 15) for a **meeting-place** for a public or official purpose: e.g. races, a conference, assembling of troops. Before **venue** came into fashion **rendezvous** was a popular word, but that was used also for a meeting arranged between two private persons.

The adjectives **truthful** and **veracious**, like the nouns **truthfulness** and **veracity**, can be applied to a person or to a statement. **veracious** and **veracity** are somewhat formal (see 15).

true, when applied to a person, means "real", "having all the attributes implied in the name" (e.g. "a true friend", "the true heir"), or "reliable" (e.g. "true as steel").

VERY, MUCH 386

C.O.D. points out that **very** is properly restricted to (1) true adjectives: "I was very sorry;" (2) adverbs: "He was very easily convinced"; (3) present participles of verbs established as adjectives: "We had a very trying time"; (4) past participles established as adjectives: "He looked at me with a very pained expression". There is no difficulty over (1), (2), and (3), but (4) involves a fine distinction. Unless a past participle has become established as an adjective careful speakers and writers will qualify it not by **very** but by some adverb like **much, greatly**, etc. "I was much (or greatly, etc.) pleased to hear the news"; not "very pleased". Treble and Vallins's *A B C of English Usage* points out that the same limitation applies to a few adjectives that are used only predicatively (not attributively): e.g. **afraid, awake, aghast**. One cannot say "He is an afraid man". Therefore one ought not to say "He was very afraid".

Apart from this, **very** is so much abused by being tacked on to adjectives almost mechanically, or to save the trouble of choosing another adjective for supplying without **very** the emphasis needed, that its edge has become blunted, and often the effect would be stronger if an adjective were left starkly bare. A well-known teacher used to advise his students never to use **very** except when they said **not very**.

The first two nouns are mostly used in the plural. **viands** means **food** at a meal, and implies variety and excellence of what is provided. The word is not often used today, but a journalist anxious to impress his readers might write of the **viands** eaten on some festive occasion. **victuals** is sometimes used facetiously: "The victuals were excellent", "Victuals were somewhat short", but the word is not properly synonymous with **food** at meals, and ought to refer to stores provided to a hotel, ship, etc.

388   VIEW, OPINION, VIEW-POINT, STANDPOINT

A **view** in its figurative use is a mental attitude, an **opinion. view-point, point of view,** and **standpoint** are used instead by those who disdain these two simple words. In a literal sense they are used in guide-books and the like.

389   VISUALIZE, ENVISAGE

The primary meaning of **envisage** is "face", "confront", with the physical eyes or figuratively. Thus the *Shorter Oxford English Dictionary* quotes Keats for this sense in 1820: "to envisage circumstances all calm". It cites an example from 1857 for the earliest date at which the word was used in its present widespread meaning of regard as probable or possible. Fowler, describing **envisage** as an "eighteenth-century word only, and a surely undesirable Gallicism", says that there are existing words equal to all requirements: e.g. **visualize, contemplate, imagine.** As he points out elsewhere, writing is not improved by stylish instead of working words. Nevertheless this frequent use of the word seems to be passing, from what in his time may have been cheap journalese, into established English. "These proposals envisage the establishment of a strong corporate government by a trusteeship council."

Two distinctions between **envisage** in this current use and visualize ("make in the mind an image of" something) are recognizable. (1) **visualize** can refer to what has happened, is happening, will or may happen, including a person's experience in the past or possible experience in the future; whereas **envisage** can refer only to the future. (2) **visualize** generally refers to material things, of which a concrete and detailed picture is formed. **envisage** generally refers to abstract concepts: e.g. political, social, economic conditions. When in *Locksley Hall* Tennyson had a prophetic foresight of the bombing aeroplane, he **visualized**

> a ghastly dew
> From the nations' airy navies grappling in the central
> blue.

He goes on to **envisage** a state of society in which there will be "a Parliament of man, the Federation of the world".

Sir Ernest Gowers in *Plain Words* includes both **envisage** and **visualize** in a list of words "overworked in official documents", and, as "useful change-bowlers", for **envisage** suggests **contemplate, face**; for **visualize** suggests **imagine, picture.**

VOCATION, AVOCATION   390

The primary meaning of **vocation** (Latin *vocare*="to call") is a divine call, or strong recognition of one's fitness for a particular form of work. "The test of a vocation is the love of the drudgery involved" (Pearsall Smith). With this meaning we speak of a person's having, feeling, showing (or not having, etc.) "a sense of vocation"—for, say, the ministry. The word is now, however, more commonly used for the profession, trade, or other work in which a person is engaged as his principal business.

avocation (Latin *avocare*="call away") is an activity in which we are not engaged in our **vocation** or chief work in life: a diversion, a distraction, a minor occupation, even if we are more interested in it than our major one; often a

hobby. It is sometimes used incorrectly as synonymous with
vocation. "A person may thus be led to neglect his everyday avocations." This meaning can be found as far back
as the seventeenth century, when the word was so used by
Robert Boyle, and the *Oxford English Dictionary* quotes
several instances among modern writers, but the usage
deprives us of a useful distinction.

391   VOICE, EXPRESS

The verb **voice** is a vogue-word (see 34) for **expresss**. Its
popularity with reference to what is spoken is no doubt due
to its conveying the idea of utterance in words. With reference to what is written this justification does not apply.
Opinions may perhaps be suitably described as **voiced** at the
Albert Hall; not suitably in an article in *The Times*. Perhaps
the fact of its having one syllable against the two of **express**
partly accounts for its frequent use.

392   VOLUME, TOME, TITLE, BOOK, WORK

The term **volume** is generally used of a **book** when the
reference is to its physical form as consisting of printed
sheets bound together: "the second volume of Macaulay's
History of England"; "a one-volume edition of Shakespeare"; "There are five thousand volumes in the library";
"It makes a handsome quarto volume".

tome, with reference to a particular **volume**, e.g. "a
weighty tome", is rarely used now except facetiously.

title has come into vogue in recent years as a piece of
trade jargon in publisher's advertisements. We read an
announcement of "six new titles" in the X series. Before
long we may be told by a publishing firm that their popular
author, Mr. A., "is now engaged on a new title, which will
recount his experiences in China in recent years". One
publisher when challenged on the usage contended that

title sometimes provided a useful distinction in the publishing and bookselling trade, but he did not explain why this convenience could not be allowed to rest in the office and the shop, instead of being introduced into advertisements addressed mainly to the general public, to whom **book** or **volume** would have no ambiguity.

work for a single **book** is pretentious. "This latest work is not marked by the clarity we are accustomed to in his treatment of economic problems." The use of the word in its literary connection is best restricted either to the complete output of an author or his writing in general: "His work is constantly marred by sentimentality"; or to a sequence of books, or a book that comprises more than one volume. "I have just finished reading the trilogy. It is a magnificent work." "This work [Macaulay's *History of England*] is in seven volumes."

WAGE, SALARY, FEE, REMUNERATION, 393 EMOLUMENT, STIPEND, BONUS, GRATUITY, TIP, HONORARIUM, PAYMENT

All the words refer to money paid for work done, and **payment** is the working word.

wage is **payment**, especially by the week, to persons doing manual or mechanical work; shop assistants; subordinate clerks, etc. (This is the only one of the words to be used figuratively. "The wages of sin is death".)

salary is fixed periodical payment, generally by the month or quarter, to employees other than those covered by **wage**: from bank-clerks, teachers, etc., to a Minister of the Crown or a highly paid managing director of an important company.

fee is payment for an individual piece of work done by a professional person.

remuneration is a general and formal word (see 15) to cover payment for any form of work.

emolument is a formal word for **salary** or **fee**.

stipend is a formal word for **salary**, especially for a clergyman's official income.

bonus is a sum of money additional to a fixed payment.

gratuity is used for a special grant: e.g. to soldiers who have served in a war; or as a formal word for **tip**: a payment to servants, railway porters, and others, for personal service.

honorarium is a voluntary payment for professional service.

394   WAKE, AWAKE, AWAKEN, WAKEN

wake is the ordinary working word in the literal sense of "cease to sleep" (intransitive) or "rouse from sleep" (transitive). It is often compounded with "up".

For an elaborate analysis of the use of the literal and figurative uses of the words see *M.E.U.*, or, for a table compiled from this, Treble and Vallins's *A B C of English Usage*.

395   WASHING, ABLUTION

ablution, except in the sense of ceremonial washing of the person or of sacred vessels, is (generally in the plural) either used facetiously or a genteelism (see 34). The genteel, feeling that a reference to cleaning the body is not quite nice in polite society (e.g. a hostess, before a meal, to her guests,) thinks to refine the effect by substituting for the short, Saxon, natural word **washing**, the longer, Latin-rooted, less common, high-sounding word **ablutions**.

396   WEIGHTY, HEAVY

weighty and **heavy** in their literal meaning, with reference to concrete objects, are closely synonymous, but **weighty** is rarely used in this way. In their figurative uses the two words are not closely synonymous. Thus **weighty** (=“important”, “authoritative”, “worthy of consideration”), but not **heavy,** would be applied to a “pronouncement”, “task”, “question”, “argument;” on the other hand **heavy,** but not **weighty,** would be applied to “loss”, “bill”, “responsibility”, “cares”.

WOOD, FOREST   397

(1) A **forest** in the most common use of the word is a large **wood**: i.e. a large tract thickly grown with trees. It may have, however, other meanings as follows. (2) A tract in which trees are mixed with pasture. (3) A tract formerly **forest** in sense (1) or (2), now cultivated, and with a proper name affixed: e.g. “The New Forest”. (4) An unenclosed tract, with few if any trees, kept as a preserve for game: e.g. the “deer forests” of the Highlands.

Those interested in etymology will find that **forest** has a strange history derived from the Latin *foris*=“out of doors,” whence came a Low Latin adjective, *forestris*; then an old French noun *forest*; and later French *forêt*.

WOOLLEN, WOOLLY   398

woollen=made of wool. **woolly**=covered with wool, or, figuratively, lacking in precision or incisiveness, especially with reference to language.

WRITE, SEND, ADDRESS   399

address as a synonym for **write** or **send,** with reference to a letter, is officialese. “Your claim will be considered as soon as possible, and a further communication will then be addressed to you.”

For **communication** see 180.

young is a general word that can refer to human beings, other living things, institutions, etc. (e.g. a "young country", a "young firm"). The three other words refer only to human beings. **youthful** is generally applied to qualities typical of **young** people: e.g. a "youthful appearance", "youthful resilience", "youthful enthusiasms". **juvenile** refers to things pertaining to **young** people: e.g. "juvenile books" in the "juvenile department" of a public library, courts for "juvenile offenders".

puerile is always used in a depreciatory sense, with reference to something done by a grown-up person that shows immaturity. Compare the use of **childish** (31).

ADDITIONAL EXAMPLES

75 DISINTERESTED, UNINTERESTED

(See p. 49). "Bonnet stated at the Munich Conference that France had shown herself disinterested in East Europe." "Over Ribbentrop's visit to Paris in 1938 the populace showed itself apathetic and uninterested."

235 PAINTER, ARTIST

(See p. 119). Peter: "It seemed to me we had a great deal in common. We are both artists." Edward: "I never thought of that. Which arts do you practise?" (T. S. Eliot: *The Cocktail Party*.)

272 PROPOSITION, PROPOSAL, PLAN

(See p. 136). "Fourscore and seven years ago our fathers brought forth a nation dedicated to the proposition that all men are created equal." (Abraham Lincoln in his Gettysburg speech.)

APPENDIX

Classified Lists of Formal Words, Show-words, Vogue-words, Genteelisms, Snob-words, Jargon, Journalese, Officialese, Commercialese, Archaisms

The classification given here, following that in the body of the book, is not rigid. No two of the five classes are always mutually exclusive. In *Modern English Usage* H. W. Fowler, who invented the terms Genteelism and Vogue-word, and first used the term Formal Word for a particular usage, himself entered some words under more than one of these headings.

The references are to the numbered articles on the word-groups.

I. FORMAL WORDS AND SHOW-WORDS

(See Group 15)

acquire, 223
aid, 139
amity, 123
anomalous, 97
apprehend, 375
apprise, 362
aroma, 336
ascertain, 74
assist, 139
attempt, 89
cast, 367
category, 26
cease, 88
cessation, 88
commence, 15
commencement, 15
comprehend, 375
conceal, 37
conclude, 349
conclusion, 88
concourse, 39
consider, 365

cryptic, 57
decease, 238
demise, 238
denominate, 24
descry, 320
designate, 24
designation, 67
devoid, 379
discern, 320
disclose, 310
display, 310
dwell, 300
emolument, 393
encomium, 259
endeavour, 89
espy, 320
eulogium, 259
eventuate, 136
evince, 310
exhibit, 310
exiguous, 100
frequently, 225

II. VOGUE-WORDS

(See Group 34)

liquidate, 186
liquidation, 186
mentality, 202
meticulous, 203
nostalgia, 219
nostalgic, 219
nostalgically, 219
overall, 232
personality, 244
personnel, 246

precondition, 262
prerequisite, 262
psychological, 274
reaction, 280
repercussion, 303
sabotage, 314
stage, 342
stress, 350
target, 361

III. GENTEELISMS AND SNOB-WORDS

(See Group 85)

ablution, 395
artist, 235
contract, 48
costly, 101
dispose, 322
donate, 127
edifice, 85
exclusive, 98
gentleman, 195
indisposed, 147
indisposition, 147
lady, 195
list, 187
mansion, 301
mental, 201

partake, 237
pass, 238
passing, 238
perfume, 336
place, 251
portion, 236
purchase, 277
remit, 294
remittance, 294
reside, 300, 301
residence, 301
retire, 308
serviette, 326
stomach, 348
tipsy, 83

IV. JARGON, JOURNALESE, OFFICIALESE, COMMERCIALESE

accrue, 304
acquire, 223
activate, 211
address, 399
advert, 287
advice, 362
advise, 362
aggravating, 169
allergic, 8

authentic, 12
beat, 366
blue-print, 252
brochure, 188
catachresis, 337
cent, 236
communication, 180
concerning, 288
contingency, 137

contract, 48
cross-section, 319
decimate, 174
develop, 136
development, 137
dispatch, 122
dwell, 300
egalitarian, 92
eventuality, 137
evince, 310
experimentation, 102
expire, 238
favour, 180
following, 118
forthwith, 148
forward, 122
gift, 127
hither, 140
indisposed, 147
indisposition, 147
inform, 362
initiate, 15
list, 187
locality, 188
mansion, 301
materialize, 136
motivate, 211
nil, 218
number, 220
obtain, 223

Occident, 224
Orient, 224
partake, 237
percentage, 236
phenomenal, 249
phenomenon, 249
prepared, 281
prior, 118
proceed, 268
procure, 223
re, 288
ready, 281
regarding, 288
register, 289
relating, 288
remit, 294
render, 297
rendition, 297
repast, 298
respecting, 288
same, 315
secure, 223
shambles, 329
spot, 341
stem, 66
superlative, 351
title, 392
transpire, 136
viand, 397
voice, 391

V. ARCHAISMS

acquaint, 362
affluent, 311
anent, 288
aver, 317
collation, 298
converse, 359
discourse, 359

divers, 114
doff, 81
don, 81
epistle, 180
ere, 93
folk, 240
forceful, 120

forthwith, 148
hither, 140
missive, 180
nigh, 214
repast, 298
save, 316

seek, 321
straightaway, 148
straightway, 148
sundry, 114
tome, 392

INDEX

The references in Arabic numerals are to the numbered articles on the word-groups.